ACHIEVEMENT FOR ALL:
Keys to Educating
Middle Grades Students
in Poverty

Ruby K. Payne, Ph.D.

Association for Middle Level Education
Westerville, Ohio

Printed in the United States of America.

ISBN: 978-1-56090-255-3

Library of Congress Cataloging-in-Publication Data

Payne, Ruby K.
  Achievement for all : keys to educating middle grades students in poverty / Ruby K. Payne, Ph.D.
    pages cm.
  Includes bibliographical references.
  ISBN 978-1-56090-255-3
  1. Children with social disabilities--Education--United States. 2. Poor children--Education--United States. 3. Educational equalization--United States. I. Title.
  LC4091.P39 2013
  371.826'94--dc23

                    2013031907

Association for Middle Level Education
4151 Executive Parkway, Suite 300
Westerville, Ohio 43081 | www.amle.org

CONTENTS

Foreword

As Executive Director of the Association for Middle Level Education (AMLE), I am proud to join with Ruby Payne in producing a book that gives educators the information they need about how poverty impacts young adolescents' physical, cognitive, social-emotional, psychological, and moral development, and how they learn. AMLE's mission is to improve the educational experiences of all students ages 10–15, so combining Ruby's expertise on educating the under-resourced with our expertise on the development of young adolescents is a natural fit.

You will find that Ruby has based her manuscript on the characteristics identified in AMLE's *This We Believe: Keys to Educating Young Adolescents* (NMSA, 2010) to guide educators in developing schools to ensure that every young adolescent becomes a healthy, productive, and ethical adult. She provides a wealth of ideas for making the education of young adolescents (1) developmentally appropriate, (2) challenging, (3) empowering, and (4) equitable. The joint message of Ruby's company, aha! Process, and AMLE is that to successfully teach under-resourced youths, you have to develop relationships with them, and to develop relationships with them, you have to understand where they come from, what their struggles are outside of school, who they are as individuals, and what their dreams are.

We know that under-resourced students at the middle level are a critical part of all strategies to achieve the national goal of graduating all students from high school prepared for a career, college, and civic life. Robert Balfanz's decade of research at Johns Hopkins and direct field experience in more than 30 middle schools showed that in high-poverty environments, a student's middle grades experience strongly impacts the odds of graduating from high school. (Balfanz, 2009). Under-resourced environments for middle grades students can result in the factors of significant, chronic absenteeism, lack of belief in hard work bringing life success, and lack of self-management, self-motivational, and organizational skills—all of which he identified as critical to middle school success.

I hope that this book will arm educators with the tools to support young adolescents in poverty to succeed in school and in life.

William D. Waidelich, EdD, CAE
Executive Director, AMLE

INTRODUCTION:
What Does It Mean To Be an Adolescent in Poverty?

The purpose of this book is to promote the development of assets and resources for students in the middle grades. We will explore what can be done when students come to school with fewer resources than they need and what educators can do to help those students develop as successful, resourced human beings.

Although many significant developments occur during early adolescence (years 10–15), the following tend to be the most important.

1. Physical development: puberty and body image

2. Cognitive/intellectual development: brain changes

3. Moral development: development of a moral compass

4. Psychological development: identity and differentiation from adults

5. Social/emotional development: safety and belonging—"fitting in"

Each of the first five chapters focuses on one of these, listing the characteristics of the type of development, reviewing the research about that stage of development, discussing how under-resourcing impacts that type of development, and finally, suggesting interventions for the under-resourcing. The sixth chapter outlines school interventions that can improve the chances of success for under-resourced students. The Conclusion emphasizes the importance to adolescents and the community of laying a strong foundation at the middle level, as well as the lasting value of excellent teachers and schools.

Throughout the book, I have drawn upon the wealth of research and resources that the Association for Middle Level Education (AMLE) provides for educators to fulfill their mission of improving the education of all students ages 10–15. Long a champion of developmentally appropriate learning, they are the perfect partner for me as I apply my own research, resources, and experience to the problem of helping all middle grades students succeed. And, although I do cite research and spend a fair amount of time giving you background knowledge about adolescent development, my aim is to provide you with real-world interventions for real-world issues.

Connecting the Factors of Environment, Resources, and Relationships

Three interlocking factors impact the cognitive framework of adolescents. First, is the environment, or surroundings. It's a well-known axiom in biology that a key to survival is for organisms, including people, to adapt to their external environments. The second factor is the availability of resources: The more stable the resources, the more predictable the environment. The more predictable the environment, the more an individual can plan and have a future story. If an individual is in an environment with scarce resources, then every day becomes a win-lose proposition for survival.

In addition to environment and resources, the cognitive framework of adolescents includes relationships (and knowledge derived from those relationships). The following diagram illustrates these three interlocking factors that impact thinking.

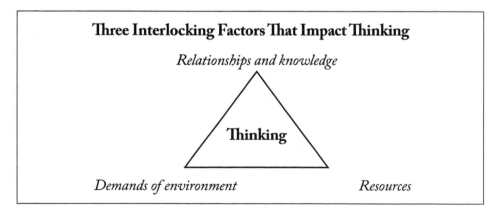

Three Interlocking Factors That Impact Thinking

Relationships and knowledge

Thinking

Demands of environment   *Resources*

In my book *A Framework for Understanding Poverty* (2013), I state that the fewer resources you have, the more you "live" on the left-hand side of the following chart. If you have more resources, the more you live on the right side of the chart.

Continuum of Resources That Help Build Stability

UNDER-RESOURCED		RESOURCED
Instability/crisis	. . . .	Stability
Isolation	. . . .	Exposure
Dysfunction	. . . .	Functionality
Concrete reality	. . . .	Abstract, representational reality
Casual, oral language	. . . .	Written, formal register
Thought polarization	. . . .	Option seeking
Survival	. . . .	Abundance
No work/intermittent work	. . . .	Work/careers/larger cause
Poverty	. . . .	Wealth
Less educated	. . . .	More educated

Source: A Framework for Understanding Poverty by R. K. Payne, 2013.

In this book, we will examine each of the above characteristics, provide a checklist for each in order to understand to what extent a student has resources, analyze the impact of that reality, and provide interventions that assist with the development of resources.

Under-Resourced Environments Can and Do Produce Strengths

You have probably heard the saying "That which doesn't kill you, only makes you stronger." Adapting to an under-resourced environment can develop valuable strengths and characteristics in many individuals, such as

- The ability to survive.
- A clear understanding of concrete reality.
- The ability to defend oneself.
- A strong sense of connection with others who also are in survival mode.
- An ability to problem-solve and "make do" with minimal materials.

- A sixth sense about adults who may not be "safe."
- The capacity for sometimes going all day without food.
- An informal, even casual, approach to living.
- The ability to entertain and be entertained.
- A capacity for enjoying the basics of life in very immediate ways.

Furthermore, just because an environment is under-resourced doesn't mean it's permanent. Note that each of us, whether we are adult or adolescent, periodically lack everything we require. Just because we may not have had all the resources that we wished for at a given time in our life doesn't mean that we were or are a failure; overcoming adversity is a part of life. And just switching external environments requires a different set of resources to survive, which then requires new adaptations and support.

The purpose of this book is simply to acknowledge the realities of under-resourced situations and then identify ways to compensate for the scarcity. Life always has been and always will be about learning and growing.

1

PHYSICAL DEVELOPMENT

In the wonderful book titled *This We Believe: Keys to Educating Young Adolescents* (National Middle School Association, 2010), the following characteristics of physical development of young adolescents are listed. (I have rephrased and simplified the original list. For added detail, see *This We Believe*.)

- Rapid, irregular physical growth
- Body changes that create awkwardness
- Varying maturity rates
- Restlessness and fatigue due to hormonal changes
- The need for daily physical activity
- The need to release energy
- Preferences for junk food
- Risky dieting practices
- Developing sexual awareness
- Concern with bodily changes
- Increased need for accurate information about sex and health
- Physical vulnerability to drugs
- High-risk sexual behaviors
- Poor habits

What Does the Research Indicate About Physical Development of Adolescents?

The biggest issue for adolescents ages 10–15 is *puberty*. And the biggest issue about puberty that concerns adolescents is simply: *Am I they going through the physical changes at about the same time as my friends?* Too early or too late, and they lose status with their peers.

There can be up to three years of variation either way in all the changes adolescents go through during puberty, depending on the genetics and ethnicity of an adolescent. The average girl is two years ahead of the average boy in height changes. A girl's height spurt generally occurs before *menarche*—the first menstrual period—but the boy's height spurt usually takes place after *spermarche*—his first ejaculation.

A young adolescent, on average, gains from two to four inches in height per year, and in weight, the gain is eight to ten pounds. Over the five year period of young adolescence, this amounts to an average gain of 10 to 20 inches in height and 40 to 50 pounds in weight (Balk, as cited in Strahan, L'Esperance, & Van Hoose, 2009). Because these increases come in irregular spurts and at varying speeds, they would be considered a medical concern in anyone other than a young adolescent. Although they give an overview, these averages do not highlight the wide range of variation in the physical development of young adolescents.

The weight gain can cause students in middle grades concern, even though the weight gain is natural and not an indication of the onset of obesity. Students may worry about the physical changes and believe there is something wrong with them (whether they are taller, shorter, bigger, or smaller) as they continually compare themselves to others. Their ongoing changes impact their self-esteem and thus all of their social relationships which can then impact their body image and eating habits

Research shows the major importance to teens of their peers' acceptance of the physical changes they are undergoing. It also shows that early onset of puberty is a huge risk factor for them and that later onset of puberty also carries risks. The following chart is a compilation of information (Berger, 2011) about some of the risk factors of early and late maturing of girls and boys.

Risk Factors in Early and Late Maturing of Girls and Boys

	EARLY MATURING	LATE MATURING
Girls	Lower self-esteem More depression Poorer body image Earlier sexual activity Higher level of pregnancy Harsh parenting Correlates to absence of biological father (Berger, 2011, p. 387) Lower grades and the likelihood of course failure in ninth grade (Crosnoe & Johnson, 2011) More vulnerable to sexual abuse (Berger, 2011)	Four times the rate of self-harm (cutting, poisoning, etc.)
Boys	More aggressive More delinquency More alcohol abuse More early sex Correlates to absence of biological father (Berger, 2011, p. 387) Lower grades and the likelihood of course failure in ninth grade (Crosnoe & Johnson, 2011)	More anxious, depressed, and afraid of sex Four times the rate of self-harm (cutting, poisoning, etc.)

Chart compiled from information in The Developing Person Through the Life Span by K. S. Berger, 2011.

Note that if a young adolescent's parents are under the stress of illness, divorce, addiction, or if they live in a violent environment, that young person is more likely to have earlier onset puberty. Early puberty correlates with earlier sexual activity and with the absence of the biological father. Scientists do not agree on whether stress causes the early puberty or whether it's caused genetically.

Sleep

Puberty also changes the biorhythm of the body. In adolescents, it changes their day/night pattern. Many adolescents, particularly males, are more alert in the evening than in the morning. Consequently, they are often sleep-deprived because they stay up late and get up early for school; they then feel sleepy during school. Females tend to be on a monthly cycle of hormonal swings, while males tend to operate on a daily cycle of hormonal swings. (In other words, male bodies often react in ways they cannot predict, causing embarrassment, fear, and shame.)

Body image

When adolescents enter puberty with all its physical and hormonal changes, they live the myth of what David Elkind (1967) called the "imaginary audience." Research indicates that they have exaggerated beliefs about others constantly observing them and negatively assessing the imperfections of their bodies. They tend also to believe that they are unique in their uneven, sometimes troubling physical changes and that they are alone and misunderstood in a world that is now unreliable. Comparison to media body types and peer body types is frequently the topic of conversation, even preoccupation.

Nutrition

Nutrients are needed for the growth of adolescents' body organs, including the stomach, and they often crave food. Gorging themselves in response, many choose fried foods, carbonated beverages, and candy, and many have diets lacking fruits and vegetables. So, although many adolescents have enough calories, they do not have the level of vitamins and nutrients that their bodies need. Iron is particularly important for females because of the loss of iron through menstruation; for males iron is essential due to the development of muscles. While the recommended daily intake of iron is 15 milligrams, only about half of U.S. adolescents get that much iron. In addition, 85% of adolescent females do not consume enough calcium.

If students seem unresponsive in the morning, they may have skipped breakfast—which will impact their academic performance and certainly their attention span. If they return from lunch with heightened alertness due to sugar, they may get sleepy before the school day is over. Students who have nutritious breakfasts and lunches will usually maintain concentration and be interactive as the lesson requires. Increasingly, schools are providing free- or reduced-cost breakfasts and lunches to help with this problem.

Because teens are so fixated on body image, which is related to nutrition, they often develop eating disorders. A combination of causes creates eating disorders—"cultural images, stress, puberty, hormones, and childhood patterns" (Berger, 2011, p. 392). As many as 7 to 8% of females in the U.S. have anorexia nervosa or bulimia across their lifetimes. In addition, girls may experiment with diet pills and boys with steroids.

Overweight and obesity with its attendant problems of lower self-esteem, type 2 diabetes, sleep apnea, bone and joint problems, and gall bladder disease are becoming more prevalent due to inactivity and poor eating habits. The Federal Interagency Forum on Child and Family Statistics (2012) shows that

> In 2009–2010, 18 percent of children ages 6–17 were obese....Poor diet quality is a major factor in the high rate of obesity among children. In 2007–2008, on average, the diets of children ages 2–17 were too high in saturated fat and sodium, had too many calories from solid fats and added sugars, and were lacking in vegetables, fruits, and whole grains...

Sexual activity

Sexual activity tends to be influenced by three principal dynamics: biology, culture, and cohort. In other words, when did I go through puberty (biology)? What messages am I listening to in my culture (parents, media, religion)? What are my friends doing (cohort)?

Early sexual activity is associated with emotional and physical health risks such as pregnancy or contracting sexually transmitted infections (STIs). Among students nationwide, the prevalence of young adolescents having sexual intercourse for the first time before age 13 held steady from 2005 to 2009 (6.2%) (Centers for Disease Control, 2011). In 2009, 46 percent of high school students reported ever having had sexual intercourse…among those who had sexual intercourse during the past 3 months, 61 percent reported use of a condom during the last sexual intercourse, and 20 percent reported the use of birth control pills to prevent pregnancy before the last sexual intercourse. (Federal Interagency Forum on Child and Family Statistics, 2012)

Other factors

Access to doctors, dentists, and education also has an effect on health. "Poverty is strongly associated with reduced access to health care and poorer health status for adolescents" (CDC, 2007, p. 10). Also, better educated people tend to have more sources of information and easier access to resources.

How Is Physical Development Impacted When the Environment is Under-Resourced?

When an adolescent lives in an under-resourced household, several things tend to happen.

1. Access to factual information about the body and the changes occurring in it is usually limited to uninformed adults and friends. Many households in poverty do not have personal computers and the Internet. Most schools limit Internet access for security and safety reasons. While many students from poverty have cell phones, they often purchase limited minutes, reserving their time for texting and phone calls. So, access to accurate information is limited. For example, a PE teacher told me that an eighth-grade girl asked her: "Is it true you can pregnant from being in a swimming pool with a boy, even if you don't touch each other?"

2. In under-resourced households, the food is usually very high in fats and "empty" carbohydrates, which tend to be cheaper than proteins, fruits, and vegetables. Under-resourced households typically have a much

smaller supply of protein. In fact, the United Nations defines poverty around the world as whether a person has protein in his/her diet on a daily basis. Only 20% of the world does. Eating protein results in increased strength and better memory because it takes longer to metabolize, and therefore, its components remain in the bloodstream for a longer periods of time.

3. Under-resourced environments have much greater levels of stress, a factor in early puberty which correlates to a higher level of teen pregnancy. Early-teen pregnancies present additional issues: Most of the babies have higher lifelong rates of medical, educational, and social problems; greater complications for the mother and baby during pregnancy; lower birth weight; and a greater incidence of postponement of prenatal care. In addition, nutritional needs are harder to meet for both baby and mother—and teen moms are often less able to nurture, which leads to bonding and attachment issues. According to Berger, "Poverty and lack of education correlate with teenage pregnancy" (2011, p. 396).

4. Getting sleep in a high-poverty household is often problematic. The household is frequently crowded. Because the TV is used to screen out other noises, it is usually quite loud. A number of people may sleep in one room, schedules are erratic (if a person works two jobs, there is constant coming and going), individuals often sleep in their clothes, and there are few alarm clocks. If there is a pattern of violence in the neighborhood or household, there's often a sense of heightened alertness to all movement, which means that the deep sleep needed for the brain to reorganize is limited. (Dreaming reorganizes the daily events in the brain.) In fact, recent research indicates that one of the reasons that obesity is increasing in adolescents is that, because hormones are reregulated during sleep, when sleep is shortened or interrupted, that reregulation doesn't occur.

5. Exercise is also problematic in high-poverty households. Space is at a premium, neighborhoods are often unsafe, and participation in sports is limited because of transportation issues and the costs of sports. Furthermore, the early training in a sport that is so evident in resourced households (e.g., golfer Tiger Woods at age 3 was more skilled than most adult golfers) seldom occurs. So by the time the adolescent is at the middle level, he feels inadequate competing against peers who have had early training. If the adolescent is expected to be the parent in the household—i.e., take care of younger siblings while the parent works two jobs—then there is precious little time for exercise. If the parent has an addiction, again, the adolescent frequently becomes the primary caregiver for the household.

According to Berger,

> Data on almost every ailment, from every nation, and every ethnic group confirm that high school graduation correlates with health. Reasons include income and residence, but even when inadequate health resources and crowded, polluted neighborhoods are taken into account, health improves with education. (2011, p. 418)

6. Visual discrimination is a key requirement for success in school, i.e., how letters are different, how numbers are different, etc. Visual discrimination is linked to the amount of color in the household and the amount of light. Typically, households in poverty are less well lit and have less contrasting color. This inhibits the development of visual discrimination. Females learn better if they can observe color and detail, and males learn best when movement is involved. So, color, movement, and light are key environmental stimuli.

7. Sexual activity is related to culture and cohorts. In resourced households, rites of passage generally have to do with getting a job or a diploma, going to college, etc. But in high poverty neighborhoods, there's incredible pressure for adolescents to be a "real man" or a "real woman," which means fathering or birthing a child. A girl at an alternative center in a school told me: "I had my baby at 14. Then I became a real woman."

8. Further, sexual abuse happens most frequently in early puberty, particularly to girls. Victims of sexual abuse often fear sexual relationships and devalue themselves lifelong.

Identifying Resources for Physical Development

When you have a student who is having difficulty with academics or behavior, using this checklist will help you determine the best interventions to make for that particular student. Identify and use the student's present strengths to build strength in the student's less developed areas. Interventions do not work if they are based on what the student does not have. Middle level students can also identify their own resources using these checklists.

Checklist for Identifying Resources for Physical Development

Has protein in his/her nutrition on a daily basis (helps with memory and physical strength)	Yes	No
Is healthy (usually free of illness)	Yes	No
Gets sufficient sleep (6–8 hours of sleep per night)	Yes	No
Brushes teeth on a daily basis (high correlation exists between dental health and general health)	Yes	No
Has health insurance and/or access to preventive healthcare	Yes	No
Can see and hear well	Yes	No
Can move his/her body by him/herself	Yes	No
Has high levels of energy and stamina	Yes	No
Can focus energy on a task	Yes	No
Is going through puberty about the same time as his/her friends.	Yes	No
Has a positive body image	Yes	No
Engages in daily exercise	Yes	No
Has unstructured time each day to exercise	Yes	No
Is physically fit	Yes	No
Is within the healthy height/weight range for his/her age	Yes	No
Has accurate information about what is happening to his/her body and the changes that are (or will be) occurring	Yes	No
Has acceptable appearance (clothes, hair, and body are clean and presentable)	Yes	No

Source: *Under-Resourced Learners: Eight Strategies to Boost Student Achievement* by R. K. Payne, 2008.

What Are Interventions Based on the Physical Development of Young Adolescents in Poverty?

1. Give students accurate factual information about how and why their bodies will change in adolescence. Health and physical education teachers can distribute and discuss the chart included earlier in this chapter about the stages of puberty. Also give it to parents. Parents who are under a lot of stress to find essentials for the survival of their families may need reminders that big changes are coming for which their support will be needed. For the students, seeing data about the wide range of variations in sexual development and a sharing of common sexual concerns of middle level students may help them gain some much-needed perspective.

2. Make certain that faculty members are aware of the sequence of puberty, the variations in the sequence, and the impact that late and especially early puberty have on students. A friend of mine who is a behavior specialist in Houston tells this story: A male student who was short in stature was in the bathroom when two other boys came in. He asked the two boys what grade they were in. They were two grade levels below him. Immediately the male student said, "I can beat you up. You know I can." Later the behavior specialist asked the male student why he had said that. The boy admitted it was because the students were younger. Then the specialist said to him, "You are short. So am I. Sometimes we want to make up for our lack of height by being verbally mean. How did it help you to be mean to those boys?" Behavior interventions such as this require a deeper understanding of puberty to help students reflect upon their behaviors and resolve to change.

3. Have students in advisory periods or health class make posters about wise food choices and how many calories are burned doing different activities. Post them in the cafeteria. It's amazing how many people don't know that 1 pound is 3,000 calories that the body didn't use. Most people overestimate the number of calories they burn and underestimate the calories they take in. Change the posters frequently through the course of the year. Poster ideas can include:

- Calories in different variations of one kind of food (e.g., hamburger, veggie burger, cheeseburger) offered in the cafeteria.
- Body mass index and the formula for calculating it.
- "Eat this instead of this" posters (in other words, an apple has 100 calories, while French fries have 400 calories).
- The value of different nutrients in the diet (Want to be tough and strong? Eat protein!).

Will students make fun of this? Absolutely! But you will be bombarding them with positive, life-giving information.

4. Make flyers/newsletters that go home to parents with information about food and adolescent development. Include a column titled: *Did You Know???* Put the information on mp3 files and DVDs. Before a pep rally, do "advertisements" about food and exercise.

5. During lunch, give students voice and choice about which activities they will do—walking, running around the track, or exercising in the gym; offer to teach them different dances, or let them teach each other dances. Keep it fun, but make students move.

6. John Ratey, author of the book *Spark: The Revolutionary New Science of Exercise and the Brain* (2008), researched physical exercise and found that requiring 45 minutes of exercise the first 45 minutes of school causes test scores to significantly increase.

7. To counter adolescents' search for the negative aspects of their body image, give them perspective by sharing research showing strangers almost always find a woman more beautiful and attractive than the woman herself does (Etcoff, Orbach, Scott, & D'Agostino, 2004; Young, 2013). According to a United Kingdom source, "Dove's new beauty campaign confirms that we are more beautiful than we think" (www.fashion.telegraph.co.uk). Students need to know that self-assessment is usually not all that accurate.

8. *Because early puberty is such a **huge risk factor**,* have counselors set up support sessions for students who go through early puberty. The counselor in one school set up support sessions in an unpredictable way so that other

students would not be easily able to identify them (sometimes meeting second period, sometimes lunch, etc.) The students discussed challenging issues they had in common. Most adolescents tend to be so self-absorbed that they believe they're the only one experiencing a particular issue or issues. Including both peers and an understanding adult can provide support for developing awareness and skills that will overcome the risks that challenge them.

9. Actively engage students within 10 minutes of the start of class. Use strategies such as Carousel, skits, and other kinesthetic activities. Middle grades students spend a lot of time sitting in their chairs, and a kinesthetic activity changes the pace and routine of the class while re-engaging students in the content. As Jill Spencer says, "They talk, they move, they create and begin to generate an enthusiasm for a topic. The process builds concrete experiences and background information that can be referred to throughout the unit" (Spencer, 2012).

2

COGNITIVE-INTELLECTUAL DEVELOPMENT

In *This We Believe: Keys to Educating Young Adolescents* (National Middle School Association, 2010), the following characteristics of cognitive-intellectual development for young adolescents are listed. (I have rephrased and simplified the original list. For added detail, see *This We Believe*.)

- Has a wide range of intellectual development
- Has increasing ability to think abstractly
- Faces decisions that require more sophisticated cognitive and social-emotional skills
- Is intensely curious with a wide range of pursuits
- Prefers active over passive learning
- Prefers to learn while interacting with peers
- Is fascinated with the world but may be relatively uninterested in academics
- Enjoys learning in real-life situations
- Is beginning to see his/her own abilities more clearly but may denigrate those abilities when in the company of peers
- Is experimenting with more sophisticated humor
- May challenge adult authority
- Is very observant of adults

What Does the Research Indicate About Cognitive/ Intellectual Development for Adolescents?

During adolescence formal, operational thought (Sharron & Coulter, 2004) begins to develop and is often introduced in school. Students, in addition to learning concrete concepts (2 pencils plus 3 pencils equals 5 pencils), learn abstract concepts (a + b = c). Another characteristic of formal operational thought is the ability to think of possibilities in addition to the current reality. This examining of possibilities is referred to as hypothetical thought. Such thinking subsequently causes adolescents to examine just about everything— often in the form of criticism—and it's verbalized as "he/she should have, could have, would have ... or this food could have, would have been better *if...* or the teacher should have, could have, would have..." In the search for possibilities, students often ignore or underestimate the practical realities of the situation, a tendency adults frequently find unrealistic and exasperating (Berger, 2011).

While in elementary school, students likely most often used inductive reasoning (going from the specific to the general); by age 14 or so (some students can do this before this age; some do it later), many students become capable of deductive reasoning (going from the general to the specific).

Increasingly, researchers believe that advanced logic is related to a dual-process model of both emotional and analytical processes. Sometimes one system is used and not the other. One may make an analytical decision in a science class and an emotional decision with a friend. Research shows that adolescents often will take unjustified risks partly due to the rudimentary nature of their analytical abilities.

Academic achievement

For many students, achievement levels fall in middle school. Puberty itself may be part of the problem. In studies of rats and other animals, learning slows down during periods of high stress and growth (Berger, 2011, p. 419). Adolescents necessarily devote a great deal of energy to growth (in all its permutations) and preoccupation with other developmental tasks.

Neurobiology and learning

In addition to the developmental processes that are occurring in the mind during adolescence, three major themes also are playing out in the brain, according to Jay Giedd (2009), a medical doctor:

(1) The number of brain cells, their connections, and receptors for chemical messengers called neurotransmitters peak during childhood, then decline in adolescence.
(2) Connectivity among brain regions increases.
(3) The balance among frontal (executive-control) and limbic (emotional) systems changes. (Giedd, 2009, para. 8)

The balance is changed as people mature in their early 20s. What does this mean in terms of the classroom?

Plasticity. First, the decline in neurotransmitters is one of the reasons the brain has "plasticity"—the ability to establish new neural pathways by forming new habits (repetitive behaviors that develop neural networks). When the brain "prunes" the neurotransmitters no longer needed, both the learning potential and the vulnerability of teens increase. This is analogous to a highway that is frequently used staying open versus one that is rarely used on which grass and then bushes grow making it unusable for travel. The brain's plasticity makes learning easier, but it also can establish early patterns that may or may not be beneficial. *In the classroom, setting habits and repetitive patterns early on can set the foundation for a great deal of learning to follow.* First Month of School!

Connectivity. Second, connectivity is the relationship between parts of the brain that work together on a task. According to Giedd, the combination of the increased speed of making connections in the brain and a decrease in recovery time before new connections are made is "roughly equivalent to a 3,000-fold increase in computer bandwidth" (2009, para. 16). *This forms the basis for learning, so the increased connectivity can make learning faster than it was in elementary school.*

Prefrontal cortex and limbic system development. The third issue is the relationship between the prefrontal cortex of the brain (executive-control) and the limbic (emotional) system. The two systems do not develop at the same time. Lawrence Steinberg of Temple University says the brain's two systems develop at different rates. The problem is that the cognitive control system (prefrontal cortex) doesn't mature until you're in your early 20s, but the sensation-seeking (limbic) system matures in early adolescence. So, while the thrill-seeking urge is at its peak, the system that controls such urges is not. It is analogous to having a racecar without brakes.

In summary, the major developments in an adolescent at the cognitive-intellectual level are: The brain begins processing information at a formal, operational level (abstract representational level), the brain itself is changing to higher processing speeds and interconnectivity, and the emotional system develops far in advance of the control system.

How Is Cognitive-Intellectual Development Impacted By An Under-Resourced Environment?

The significant ways that poverty and under-resourced environments impact cognitive-intellectual development are in the realms of vocabulary, abstract representational systems, the ability to ask questions, and prefrontal cortex issues.

For a person living in a survival environment, everyday reality is an environment of sensory-based information and non-verbal reactions. School and work environments, however, involve plans, words, papers, and computers. The two environments are very different.

Vocabulary

Betty Hart and Todd Risley (1995) did a study for three years in which they placed tape recorders in both welfare and professional households. Their goal was to see how much language children were exposed to between the ages of 1 and 4. In welfare households children heard a total of 13 million words in three years, but in professional households the children heard a total of 45 million words. The research showed that a 3-year-old in a professional household had more vocabulary than an adult in a welfare household.

Being able to name things, ideas, feelings, etc., is vitally important when living in an abstract representational system. The brain uses names to access information—and the greater the level of specificity of vocabulary, the greater the level of brain prowess available. For students in under-resourced environments, vocabulary is often quite limited, as the Hart and Risley (1995) study confirms.

Abstract representational systems or formal operations

To do well in middle school, a student must be able to live and function effectively using representational systems. Examples of representation are: a grade represents achievement, an address on paper represents a location, a deed represents a property, and a number represents a quantity. Numbers, time, and space assign order and value to the universe. Fractions are an abstract way of representing space (how much of the pizza is yours). In science, the drawing of a cell represents the cell but is not the cell itself. A map represents space but is not that space. Because there's very little print in high-poverty households (other than what is on purchased food), students from these homes usually have scant familiarity with printed word and numbers, so they have further to go to even start conceptualizing representational systems. In poverty, time is often kept emotionally—how it feels. But in school, time is kept abstractly—minutes, hours, days.

Ability to ask questions syntactically

Many students use only casual or heritage language and come to school without the skill of posing questions in syntactically correct form. For example, they might use a voice inflection to ask, "Your homework done?" The formal, syntactical way of asking it puts the verb before the subject (Is your homework done?) What questions do is allow people to get inside their brain, think deeply, and find out what they do and do not know. Palincsar and Brown (1984) found that students who cannot ask questions syntactically rarely get past the third-grade reading level. Related to the ability to ask questions syntactically are the ability to organize information into a framework that can be consulted when categorizing new information, encouraging curiosity to engage and stay engaged with content, and setting a purpose for reading.

In high-stress, low-income households, children are often slapped for asking questions because it's viewed as disrespectful of adults. In educated, resourced households, children are encouraged to ask questions. Question-making is the tool to get inside the brain and find information—rather like a Google search. If you are slapped for asking questions, you learn not to ask them.

Prefrontal cortex issues

The prefrontal cortex of the brain does "executive functioning," which involves planning and working memory (holding information in your head while you work on one piece of it.) Examples include: doing a three-step process and while you are doing the first step, you are also remembering the second and third ones); and reward analysis (analyzing whether the reward is worth the risk and postponing gratification).

Usually the pre-frontal cortex of the brain gets developed late in adolescence, but adolescents who are in survival-of- the-fittest environments that cause them to be perpetually highly reactive, don't develop the prefrontal cortex in a normal fashion. In environments where every day is a hunt for resources to stay alive, planning, impulse control, and working memory are not rewarded or reinforced. What is rewarded is immediate survival. In a 2009 study done at the University of California/Berkeley, the brains of 9- and 10-year-olds from poverty were compared, via EEG (electroencephalogram) brain scanners, with 9- to 10-year-olds from the middle class. Researchers headed by Mark Kishi-yama found most of the adolescents from poverty produced abnormal scans of the executive function portion of their brains. Their images looked similar to those of patients with medically caused neurological issues (Kishiyama, Boyce, Jimenez, Perry, & Knight, 2009).

Working memory. Part of the prefrontal cortex controls working memory, a key factor in beginning to learn anything. Ruth Colvin Clark in her 2008 book on expertise, *Building Expertise: Cognitive Methods for Training and Performance Improvement* (3rd edition), found that for a beginning learner, the limit regarding the introduction of new concepts, ideas, etc., is generally two to four things. Working memory is a bit like a long-necked bottle—very narrow, and only a few things can get in, and then it is stuffed. Added to that is the fact that working memory has only two "folders" to accept new information—one visual and one auditory. So, for example, asking students to watch a Power-Point, listen to the teacher, and take notes leads to divided, even fragmented, attention (because there are now three methods for intake of information), and achievement drops. Added to that, students in poverty often perceive much of the material as abstract and foreign and coming at them in an overwhelming amount and at a high speed. According to Clark, a student learns more effectively by highlighting printed notes while listening to the teacher (two sources of input) and if the teacher formatively assesses the entire class for understanding as the lesson progresses.

Planning and processes. When the prefrontal cortex is undeveloped, a person has trouble planning and setting procedures for accomplishing goals. Like understanding *why* something is important in learning, the concept of *how to do* something is also very important.

Identifying Resources

When you have a student who is having difficulty with academics or behavior, using this checklist will help you determine the best interventions to make for that particular student. Identify and use the student's present strengths to build strength in the student's less developed areas. Interventions do not work if they are based on what the student does not have. Middle level students can also identify their own resources using this checklist.

Checklist for Identifying Cognitive and Intellectual Resources

Can read at a rate that doesn't interfere with meaning	Yes	No
Can read the material required for that grade level or task	Yes	No
Can write for the task as required by school or work	Yes	No
Can add, subtract, multiply, and divide	Yes	No
Can do the math as required by the grade level/course	Yes	No
Understands money as represented on paper— checkbooks, bank statements, etc.	Yes	No
Can operate in the paper and computer world of school and work	Yes	No
Can use specific vocabulary related to the academic content or the job	Yes	No
Is test-savvy—knows how to take a test	Yes	No
Can develop questions about content or tasks on the job	Yes	No
Is organized and can find papers when they're needed (paper representation of space)	Yes	No
Can read a map	Yes	No
Is able to engage in procedural self-talk	Yes	No
Can follow written directions	Yes	No
Can sequence a task or make a plan	Yes	No
Can represent an idea visually or with a story (mental models)	Yes	No
Can prioritize tasks	Yes	No
Can sort what is and is not important in a task or a text (summarization)	Yes	No
Can divide tasks into parts	Yes	No
Can get tasks or projects done on time (paper representation of time)	Yes	No
Can make to-do lists or use a planner to get things done	Yes	No
Can use a calendar	Yes	No
Can tell how things are alike and different	Yes	No
Can use formal register in the language of the dominant culture	Yes	No
Can tell a story in chronological order	Yes	No
Can get to the point in a discussion	Yes	No
Can resolve a conflict using language	Yes	No
Can ask questions using correct syntax	Yes	No
Can write using formal organizational patterns for writing	Yes	No
Can use specific vocabulary in both speech and writing	Yes	No
Can sort what is and is not important in non-fiction text	Yes	No
Can write a persuasive argument using support and logic	Yes	No

Source: *Under-Resourced Learners: Eight Strategies to Boost Student Achievement* by R. K. Payne, 2008.

What Interventions Can Help with Cognitive-Intellectual Development?

The following interventions can make a huge difference in the classroom. The book *Research–Based Strategies: Narrowing the Achievement Gap for Under-Resourced Students* (Payne, 2009) at www.ahaprocess.com provides more information about all these strategies.

1. Give students step sheets. These teach the steps and procedures for getting tasks done.

2. Use mental models. Use stories, analogies, movements, and drawings that translate from the concrete and sensory to the abstract. Here's an example of a mental model:

   In math you can show a square number physically forming a square. Nine is a square number.

    Using the mental model makes it easy to understand the root of a square. The square root of 9 is 3 because no matter how you draw straight lines through the Xs, it will always go through 3 of them.

3. Make sure that every lesson contains the what (vocabulary), the *how* (process) and the *why* (meaning). Those three things are absolutely necessary for learning anything well.

4. Monitor how much working memory you are asking students to use at once. When new ideas or concepts are being introduced, limit the new information to no more than four things and be certain only two methods of taking in information are being used (e.g., visual, auditory, kinesthetic).

5. Direct-teach vocabulary by teaching roots, suffixes, and prefixes. See www.ahaprocess.com for Donyall Dickey's (2013) graphic organizers and instructional snapshots for common core standards. Studies have shown that the vocabulary tool alone raises test scores 6–7 points in one year.

6. Make sure that students have a future story—or use what Paul Tough calls "mental contrasting" (Tough, 2012, p. 92). Ask students what intentions they have for implementing their future goals—ask students not only to identify what they want their future to be but also the obstacles that might get in the way, as well as how to deal with those obstacles.

7. Most students from poverty simply will not learn if there is not a relationship of mutual respect with the teacher. Mutual respect involves three things: support, insistence, and high expectations. Learning, particularly for under-resourced students, is double-coded—both by the nature of the relationship and by the content. If you had a teacher in school whom you hated, chances are you still don't like that subject or topic very much. On the other hand, a positive relationship with a teacher can make all the difference. James Comer (1995), a Yale University professor, has stated, "No significant learning occurs without a significant relationship."

8. Take time to engage each student in thinking about what they are reading while they are reading and help students identify when they are getting lost so they can ask a question before going on. Jill Spencer, in her book *Ten Differentiation Strategies for Building Common Core Literacy* (AMLE, 2013) provides a wealth of strategies for such formative assessment. Working in pairs or small groups to summarize information allows the students to review their thinking and gain practice in articulating their ideas to their classmates while teachers can observe how students are processing the lessons and plan for necessary interventions.

9. Use the steps from the Gradual Release of Responsibility model
    a. I do it
    b. We do it together.
    c. You do it.

10. If you are teaching students to master standards that call for analyzing, interpreting, delineating, and evaluating, remember that students in your classes will likely fall in a range of ability to handle such abstract concepts. This does not mean that some students will not have to master these skills, but they will need tools, processes, and practices that help them work through the necessary thinking steps. Some strategies could include:

- Provide or construct with students kid-friendly definitions for each of the processes. Some students don't know what the words mean, and the first step is ensuring students understand the terms.

- Teach students key vocabulary words that signal they are being asked to do a specific type of thinking (example: Analyze = categorize, infer, compare, examine). Keep a chart in the room or a digital one they can access 24/7.

- Help students identify what they might do to demonstrate they can analyze, synthesize, etc.

- Provide many non-graded practices of the process in the standards. (Spencer, 2008)

MORAL DEVELOPMENT

In *This We Believe: Keys to Educating Young Adolescents* (National Middle School Association, 2010), the following characteristics of moral development in young adolescents are listed. (I have rephrased and simplified the original list. For added detail, see *This We Believe.*)

- Transitions from a framework of "what's in it for me" to a framework that takes others and the larger culture into consideration
- Begins to see moral matters in shades of gray but may not evidence this growth yet in actual practice
- Believes in ideals
- Shows compassion for animals or individuals who are suffering
- Shows beginnings of engagement in participatory democracy
- Shows impatience with the pace of change
- Believes in values of honesty and responsibility but may not yet practice them consistently
- Sees flaws in others, but not necessarily in himself or herself
- Shows an interest in exploring spiritual matters
- Moves from accepting adult moral judgments to developing his or her own
- Relies on significant adults for advice; greatly influenced by adults who listen to him or her
- Sees the disparity between what many adults say they value and how the adults actually live

What Does the Research Indicate About Moral Development of Adolescents?

Lawrence Kohlberg (1981, 1984) identified three levels and six stages of moral reasoning. In Level 1, Preconventional Moral Reasoning, the ego-centric, self-absorbed level, the goal is to get rewards and avoid punishment. The first stage he described as "might makes right"; a stage of appearing obedient to authority and avoiding punishment, while remaining self-centered. The second stage of this level he described as "look out for number one" or be nice to others so they will be nice to you.

Level II is Conventional Moral Reasoning, the community-centered level. Stage three is people-pleasing behavior for social approval; children observe adults and try to follow the norms. Stage four is "law and order" when children follow the laws and society's rules.

When adolescents get to Level III, Postconventional Moral Reasoning, they begin to question why things are the way they are. This level is centered on moral principles and ideals. Stage five involves the social contract; social rules are obeyed because they benefit everyone. Under some circumstances disobeying the law is moral. Stage six involves universal ethical principles rather than individual (Level I) or community practices (Level II).

In Kohlberg's research he found that peer experiences help move students from preconventional to conventional reasoning. It is with intellectual maturity that adolescents are then able to move to the postconventional level. As with any developmental work, not all adolescents arrive at a level at the same time. Researchers have shown that part of moral reasoning is develop- mental and part is induced by the environment.

Criticisms of Kohlberg. Critics of Kohlberg cite the lack of accounting for gender and cultural differences and the idea that though children's morals differ from those of adults, they may be equally valid (and thus, postconventional in some ways). But, Berger (2011) states,

In one respect, however, Kohlberg was undeniably correct. Children use their intellectual abilities to justify their moral actions." This was shown in an experiment in which trios of children aged 8 to 18 had to decide how to divide a sum of money with another trio of children. Some groups chose to share equally; other groups were more selfish. There were no differences in the actual decisions, but there were age differences in the arguments voiced. Older children suggested more complex rationalizations for their choices, both selfish and altruistic. (Gummerum et al., 2008, as cited in Berger, 2011, p. 371)

Dahl (2004), quoted in Monastersky (2007), states:

Values learned during adolescence are more likely to endure than those learned later, after brain connections are firmly established…Adults should provide "scaffolding and monitoring" until adolescent brains can function well on their own. (Berger, 2011, p. 403)

In a 2005 study by C. Smith, 71% of U.S. adolescents said they believed in God, heaven, hell, and angels. They were typically in alignment with their parents' beliefs (Berger, 2011, p. 416). But they were quite egocentric about their beliefs, often seeing them as a tool for them personally in their daily life to deal with difficulties and to keep them from doing "bad things."

One of the things that adolescents do to develop their own moral codes and separate themselves from their parents, which is a very necessary developmental step (sometimes called individuation), is to question virtually everything. First-born children usually have more parent-child conflict during adolescence than do second- or later-born children, as parents also are learning to be parents (Shanahan, McHale, Osgood, & Crouter, 2007, as reported by Crosnoe and Johnson, 2011).

MaryAdele Revoy, who does research and gives presentations on adolescent brain development, highlighted some of the practical issues of the development of adolescent thinking as they examine real-life issues in a blog posting in 2011. She told about a mother who confessed to shooting and killing her children [Beau, 13 and Calyx, 16] for "repeatedly talking back to her and being 'mouthy.'"

How many parents/caregivers complain about mouthy kids?...Adolescents are known to talk back, have strong opinions, test their boundaries, and question authority. It is all part of being an adolescent who is on the journey to adulthood.

During adolescent brain development, youths develop their thinking… Five thinking areas have been identified: (1) reasoning/problem solving; (2) decision making/hypothetical situations; (3) processing information/efficiency; (4) expertise/use of experience; and (5) moral reasoning/social cognition.

For adolescents to become thoughtful, successful contributors to a community, they must develop all of these areas, and move from concrete thinking to more complex, analytical thinking. Revoy goes on to say that adults are probably most challenged with handling adolescents' struggle to understand social conventions (laws, rules, guidelines, etc.).

Why are things a certain way? Teenagers may say: *"Why do I have to be home at 11 pm when my friends can stay out to midnight?" "Why do I have to go to church when I don't believe in God anymore?" "I think my bedroom is clean enough."* The problem is that adults think questioning of social conventions as being more argumentative and direct questioning of their authority. What I like to tell the audience is that the adolescent is not becoming more argumentative, just better at it. (2011)

In moral development, an indicator of a developing adolescent is the move from egocentric thinking to being other-oriented. In a study in Canada, adolescents viewed individuals who were mean and harmful as immature. (Galambos, Barker, & Tilton-Weaver, 2003). In other words, adolescents had enough moral development to know when others did not. Other-oriented moral judgment and pro-social behaviors (helping, sharing, comforting) are indicators of movement toward a morally functioning adult. In addition, young adolescents become aware of and deeply concerned with issues of justice.

I am reminded of my son at 14 having a justice orientation to a moral issue. One of the older high school students who came from a very religious family committed suicide because he had gotten his girlfriend pregnant. My son was livid—not due to religious or moral reasons about suicide but because the student had left the girl alone with the baby to take care of the child by herself. My son said to me, "What a coward! How unfair to leave the girl to face it herself!" My son did not translate it as a religious issue or a moral issue: he translated it as a justice issue—fairness.

In *Adolescents, Families, and Social Development: How Teens Construct Their Worlds,* Judith Smetana writes:

> Along with their understanding of fairness, adolescents showed a greater capacity to incorporate ambiguous aspects of moral situations as they got older. For example, in considering direct harm in conflict situations (such as hitting in response to provocation), many children thought that it was permissible to hit back and that one should be able to engage in "self-defense" in these situations. More 10- to 14-year-olds than 8- and 16-year-olds thought that they had the right to self-defense in response to hitting. But when the child who hit first was described as emotionally vulnerable, the moral acceptability of hitting in self-defense disappeared.
>
> Moral thinking did not progress in a linear fashion. Rather, there was a U-shaped pattern of moral growth in children's and adolescents' judgments and in their ability to integrate divergent aspects of situations. There were periods of transition in teenagers' thinking. Adolescents (14-year-olds) were more able than younger children to consider aspects of moral situations, but they applied moral criteria unevenly and with uncertainty. During this transitional period, adolescents attended to new features of moral situations and groped towards more complex integrations of moral thought. In particular, in early to middle adolescence, their attempts to establish boundaries of personal jurisdiction resulted in an over-application of conceptions of rights in morally ambiguous contexts. They were "blinded" by the personal aspects of situations and gave more weight to personal prerogatives and personal goals in early to middle adolescence relative to preadolescence or late adolescence. (2010, pp. 261–262)

What Happens to Moral Development in an Under-Resourced Environment?

First of all, the fewer the resources in an environment, the more difficult it will be for individuals to get their needs met, which can impact moral development if the individual does not follow moral conventions or the law. Directly competing for scarce resources may make the choices so stark that morality and/or legality are not considered. For example, if I am truly hungry, I will probably steal food to stay alive. If I have to kill someone in order to stay alive myself, I will kill someone. If I have to lie to protect someone who is keeping me alive, I will lie. A principal in Corpus Christi told me about one of his seventh graders who wanted to be a gang member. As a test of his loyalty, part of his gang initiation was to kill a member of his family. He could not do it so he killed himself.

In discussing the moral development of young adolescents in under-resourced environments, it is helpful to review Maslow's (1943) hierarchy of needs, which shows basic needs must invariably be met first.

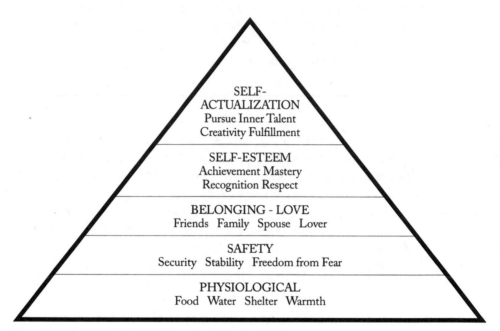

SELF-ACTUALIZATION
Pursue Inner Talent
Creativity Fulfillment

SELF-ESTEEM
Achievement Mastery
Recognition Respect

BELONGING - LOVE
Friends Family Spouse Lover

SAFETY
Security Stability Freedom from Fear

PHYSIOLOGICAL
Food Water Shelter Warmth

Source: McLeod, S. A. (2007). Maslow's Hierarchy of Needs - Simply Psychology.

Survival and justice systems *The closer people are to survival, the harsher and more immediate the systems of justice are.* In the American system of justice, people on juries debate what happens to other people. This is not the case in survival. If I have to work all day just to have enough food for myself, then every able person in my family has to work. There is no time to debate what happens to someone else. For many students from poverty, justice is both immediate and rigid. Everything is win/lose. Why? It's about survival.

In the recent past, the economy has plunged more and more formerly middle class families into times of food and home insecurity. In 2010, children in 9.8% of homes with children (3.9 million households) experienced food insecurity at times (Coleman-Jensen, Nord, Andrews, & Carlson, 2011). If people are homeless, they may be not only hungry but also lack stability in other areas of their lives. The simple reality is this: Being "moral" is much easier when your stomach is full, you know where you're going to sleep tonight, and your friends are OK.

And in some homes, even those with stable resources, children aren't allowed to argue with their parents or discuss crucial topics. How do you form your own moral codes if (a) you haven't had the chance to question them with knowledgeable adults, (b) most of the adults in the household (including, on occasion, sociopaths, addicts, and borderline personalities) have few moral guidelines, and (c) your experience base is very limited?

Distrust of the justice system. Last, in under-resourced households, the larger justice system doesn't necessarily help them and it often hurts them. So there's deep distrust of institutions and society at large. For example, foster children cannot learn to drive in the state of Florida. When they turn 18 and are ejected from the foster system, they're on their own—most not knowing how to drive. Another example is that undocumented immigrant students are not allowed to work for a living in a legitimate business in many states. People on probation must complete absolutely horrendous paperwork *and* must pay to see their probation officers.

So the concepts of fairness, justice, and win-win that are the basic constructs of schools are often foreign to high-poverty neighborhoods.

Identifying Resources for Moral Development

When you have a student who is having difficulty with academics or behavior, using this checklist will help you determine the best interventions to make for that particular student. Identify and use the student's present strengths to build strength in the student's less developed areas. Interventions do not work if they are based on what the student does not have. Middle level students can also identify their own resources using this checklist.

Checklist for Identifying Resources for Moral Development

Can evaluate situations for justice and/or moral issues	Yes	No
Has hope for the future (i.e., believes that the future will work out in a positive way)	Yes	No
Believes in the personal ability to impact his/her own life (i.e., does not believe he/she is simply fated)	Yes	No
Believes that there is extra support to help one with life (e.g., divine guidance, a set of beliefs, prayer, meditation, etc.)	Yes	No
Has a strong personal belief system about his/her own positive value as a human being	Yes	No
Feels that he/she is safe and has a sense of belonging within a group	Yes	No
Can identify how another person would feel in a given situation	Yes	No
Engages in sharing, comforting, empathy, listening to others	Yes	No
Can give moral arguments for and against a given behavior	Yes	No
Can articulate why society needs rules and norms	Yes	No

Source: *Under-Resourced Learners: Eight Strategies to Boost Student Achievement* by R. K. Payne, 2008.

The research on hope indicates that it is a huge factor in resiliency. Spiritual faith has been a marker for resiliency in the research and over time.

What Interventions Can Help with Moral Development?

1. Offer community service and volunteer opportunities. Be sure to consider the supports that need to be in place so that students from poverty have transportation to the event and students with caretaking responsibility outside of school have care provided if they are gone when it is time for the caretaking. Many schools have community projects, but the supports that under-resourced students would need in order to participate often aren't available. Being involved in service-learning projects increases students' self-esteem, helps them gain problem-solving skills, engages them academically, and has a positive impact on personal and interpersonal development.

2. Have older students mentor younger students. In the research, this made a huge difference in the achievement for both younger *and* older students. Part of moral development is one's ability to see the world from another person's point of view. Mentoring does that because it is so personal.

3. Use a restorative (rather than retributive) justice approach to discipline. The book *Restorative Justice Pocketbook* by Margaret Thorsborne and David Vinegrad (2009) is fabulous in explaining this concept (www.teacherspocketbooks.co.uk).

4. Develop assignments that allow for healthy debate and, yes, argument. In the book *The Growth of the Mind and the Endangered Origins of Intelligence*, Greenspan and Benderly (1997) identify arguing as one of the best tools for learning because it engages the emotions and is remembered longer. For help with planning a role-play debate, see *Authentic Assessment: Active, Engaging Product and Performance Measures* by Sandra Schurr (2012). Participating in a debate gives students practice in oral presentation and strengthens leadership and problem-solving skills.

5. As part of advisory periods, discuss moral, ethical, and legal dilemmas. For example, does the digital re-creation on a video of a deceased person by someone else belong by copyright to the dead person or to the person who created it? When Topac, a rap star who died, was digitally brought back to a "live video", there was a legal battle over who owned the copyrights to that video.

    Another example: If a person is hungry and has no food, is it morally justifiable to steal food from someone who has it? In history and social studies, why is the victor in a war usually morally exonerated while the country that lost is considered morally wrong? One illustration: Stalin, leader of the victorious Soviet Union in World War II, killed millions of Germans and his own people but was not convicted as a war criminal as Hitler of Nazi Germany would have been had he lived.

4

PSYCHOLOGICAL DEVELOPMENT

In *This We Believe: Keys to Educating Young Adolescents* (National Middle School Association, 2010), the following characteristics of psychological development of young adolescents are listed. (I have rephrased and simplified the original list. For added detail, see *This We Believe*.)

- Often has a preoccupation with self
- Seeks to become increasingly independent but continues to need supports and boundaries
- May give greater importance to ethnic identity
- Fluctuates in levels of self-esteem
- Gets passionately involved with at least one talent/interest/hobby
- Believes that personal problems and feelings are unique to himself/herself
- Has high sensitivity to personal criticism
- Desires recognition
- Has intense concern about physical changes
- Takes on a sexual identity
- Is curious about sex
- Is vulnerable psychologically
- Is resilient and generally optimistic about the future

What Does Research Indicate about Psychological Development for Adolescents?

Most young adolescents are preoccupied with themselves and what others think of them. David Elkind (1967) refers to this as "adolescent egocentrism." Occurring in both genders and in all ethnicities, it happens in part because of the maturation process going on inside the brain.

This adolescent egocentrism causes most adolescents to have an inflated, even melodramatic, view of themselves, their significance, and their role in the world. They feel as though no one has their problems (including self-esteem problems) and that they are unique. Elkind (1967) identifies several aspects of adolescent egocentrism to include the *personal fable* (the belief that he/she will be famous, adored, worshiped, legendary) and the *invincibility fable* (regardless of his/her behavior, no harm will occur).

The young adolescent's egocentrism causes him or her to create an "imaginary audience," who watches, critiques, and pays attention to everything the individual does (Berger, 2011, p. 409). This imaginary audience makes the adolescent even more self-conscious. What this audience does more than anything else is *judge* the adolescent—and so, during the day, any incident, innocuous or with intent, impacts the adolescent either for better or for worse— "Oh, he looked at me" (interpretation: *I must be beautiful*) or "Oh, he ignored me" (interpretation: *I must be ugly*). The imaginary audience obscures any reality checks. The adolescent, therefore, literally careens through the day in response to this imaginary audience. This self-absorbed psychological experience feeds into and helps develop adolescent identity.

Identity

Part of the human quest for meaning is to determine *Who am I?* And adolescents are no different. During early adolescence there's a strong desire to find a niche with friends and develop close relationships with them. It's part of the individuation from parents that must occur in order to become an adult. Erik Erikson (1968) writes that finding identity is the primary task of adolescence; he is credited with coining the phrase "identity crisis." As this process of finding identity is taking place, Erikson identifies "role confusion"—i.e., the complicated, often conflict-inducing task of finding out who you are and separating from parents, other adults, and friends. Erickson holds that role confusion is addressed by having "identity achievement"—figuring out the beliefs, values, talents, and culture that you wish to keep as your own.

It's during this period that adolescents are most prone to argue with and challenge adults. Because their negotiating skills and vocabulary may not have the conceptual frames necessary for more sophisticated arguments, the discussions often become muddied with accusation, criticism, and blame. Bickering and nitpicking with adults become frequent occurrences. Adolescents' seeking their identities is often shown as they argue, try out different points of view, and explore the areas of religion, politics, gender, ethnicity, and socialization.

There are four principal ways that adolescents deal with identity development: diffusion, foreclosure, moratorium, and achievement.

- **Diffusion** means that the confusion is intense, so adolescents are often overwhelmed and simply engage in avoidance activities (gaming, TV watching, sleeping, etc.).
- **Foreclosure** means they stop questioning and simply accept the traditional values without further questioning.
- **Moratorium** means they take a "time out." (For example, college is a moratorium of sorts where one is allowed to experiment with many ideas and experiences without making a long-term decision.)
- **Achievement** means that some sort of understanding of self is determined.

In other words, when adolescents are immersed in figuring out just who they are and what they believe, they can become so intensely involved and passionate that they get overwhelmed and take refuge in avoidance activities such as sleeping, sports, gaming, TV watching, using digital devices, etc., and then pick up the struggle later. They may choose to keep on trying out options without making a long-term decision, or they may just stop questioning the issue altogether and accept the traditional values. And, of course, they may find and understand their identity and "live" it for a long, long time or forever. Perhaps you know a person who decided they were a vegetarian, a follower of a different religion from his or her parents, a social activist, or a runner in middle school and then never wavered from that position.

This identity process is repeated all of one's life, but it generally first begins in adolescence.

Bonding/separation/individuation

There is a cycle that most of us repeat numerous times in our lives for many reasons. It is the bonding/separation/individuation cycle. We do it as a child in relationship to a parent; we do it as a parent in relationship to a child; we do it in the workplace; we do it as we age; we do it as we move spiritually, emotionally, and mentally along life's path.

Part of reaching adulthood emotionally well is (1) having a strong bond with a caretaker, (2) separating as a distinct person in the context of that bond (e.g., the 2-year-old who constantly says no), and then (3) individuating as one's own person. Then we typically bond to something or someone new (see the figure, "Bonding, Separation, Individuation Cycle"). As noted above, we tend to repeat this pattern our entire life.

- It happens in marriages. There is the initial bonding, then separating/distancing, then (if the marriage stays intact) individuating by each person in the couple.

- It happens in the workplace. Most of us need to feel a sense of belonging in order to stay in a particular career and be happy there. Then we identify how our values and priorities are not like the workplace, and we separate from it, usually figuratively. Then within the workplace we decide what we will and won't do—and to the degree we will and won't do it. Sometimes this process results in quitting a job and looking for another one.

- It happens as a part of dying. We bond to individuals, but as we age, many of our friends die. The separation is often painful. It induces us to individuate. Then, ideally, we're able to bond with new friends, gain new learnings, and adapt to new situations.

Bonding, Separation, Individuation Cycle

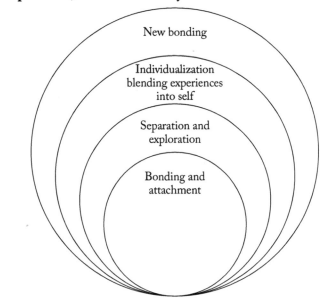

Source: How Much of Yourself Do You Own? A Handbook for Developing Emotional Resources by R. K. Payne, in press)

At each stage of this cycle, emotional adjustments and new understandings are required. Not counting the "terrible twos," the first movement from bonding to individuation begins in earnest during adolescence and shapes the future of many of our students. If parents or adults are too controlling, then one of three things tends to happen. The adolescent:

- Rebels
- Becomes passive-aggressive
- Becomes co-dependent upon the parent/adult

Success is related not just to identity and role but also to persistence, engagement, and motivation. Will I stick with it? Am I engaged when I do it? (Is it more fun than work?) Will I do it without prompting?

Persistence, engagement, and motivation

"Persistence, engagement, and motivation seem more crucial than intellectual ability in finishing school," says Berger (2011, p. 428). Carol Dweck (2006), in her book *Mindset: The New Psychology of Success*, a compilation of 25 years of research, found that if students believe that it takes hard work to learn and to achieve, then they achieve a lot more than the students who consider themselves "smart."

Paul Tough (2012), in his book *How Children Succeed: Grit, Curiosity and the Hidden Power of Character*, argues that it's about "character," which he defines as persistence, self-control, curiosity, conscientiousness, grit, and self-confidence. Tough says there are a least two windows of opportunity for change: early childhood and early adolescence. He states, "If we can improve a child's environment in the specific ways that lead to better executive functioning, we can increase his prospects for success in a particularly efficient way" (p. 21).

What Happens to Psychological Development When the Household is Under-Resourced?

Many social scientists identify adulthood as becoming an employee, a partner/spouse, and a parent. Some adolescents, particularly from low-income and under-resourced households, become an "adult" very young—skipping the developmental stages of adolescence. This is particularly damaging.

In most under-resourced households, students experience different psychological development. Annette Lareau (2003), in her book *Unequal Childhoods: Class, Race, and Family Life*, identifies the way class impacts how children are raised and their future lives. She studied black and white households in both poverty and the middle class and found that the differences in how children were raised had more to do with class than race.

In her work Lareau found that middle class households raised their children in a "concerted cultivation" while poverty households allowed for "natural growth."

Middle class households enrolled their children in sports and after school activities, they coached their children how to negotiate with authorities, and they "cultivated development" of their children. In poverty households, children were left "on their own." When the parents went to school with an issue, it was more to complain than to negotiate.

Typology of Differences in Child Rearing

	Child Rearing Approach	
	Concerted Cultivation	**Accomplishment of Natural Growth**
Key Elements	Parent actively fosters and assesses child's talents, opinions, and skills.	Parent cares for child and allows child to grow
Organization of Daily Life	Multiple child leisure activities orchestrated by adults	"Hanging out," particularly with kin, by child
Language Use	Reasoning/directives Child contestation of adult statements Extended negotiations between parents and child	Directives Rare questioning or challenging of adults by child General acceptance by child of directives
Interventions in Institutions	Criticisms and interventions on behalf of the child Training of the child to take on this role	Dependence on institutions Sense of powerlessness and frustration Conflict between child-rearing practices at home and school
Consequences	Emerging sense of entitlement on the part of the child	Emerging sense of constraint on the part of the child

Source: *Unequal Childhoods: Class, Race, and Family Life* by Annette Lareau (2003), p. 31.

In middle-class households, according to Lareau's studies, children were taught how to navigate institutions and advocate for themselves with adults as necessary. In most poor households, adolescents were not taught to question adults and, as they became adults, felt a sense of constraint or limitation as human beings because they lacked the negotiation skills. The table above summarizes Lareau's findings.

Biochemical issues.

Mental illness (biochemical issues) and addiction are very prevalent issues in poverty. Research shows that about 3% of households in middle class have a mental health issue versus about 7% in poverty. There's a great deal of discussion in the literature about which came first—mental illness causing poverty or poverty causing stress and eventually mental illness. The reality in poverty is this: Because resources are so scarce in the culture of survival, many individuals self-medicate. Getting drunk is cheaper than going to the psychiatrist. Note that addiction is prevalent in all classes, but it is typically addressed differently because the resources are different. Addiction to medication is pervasive in the middle class, but it is legal. Health insurance pays for the doctor visits and the medication. In wealthy households, staff is hired to assist the person with the addiction.

A wonderful book, *Help Me, I'm Sad: Recognizing, Treating, and Preventing Childhood and Adolescent Depression* (Fassler & Dumas, 1997), gives excellent information about adolescents with biochemical issues and ways to address them. Note that many adolescents who do consult doctors about biochemical issues tend to quit taking prescribed medicines once they feel better, although they are supposed to continue their medications. Another factor in addressing biochemical issues is the difficulty of stabilizing the medicines due to the changing hormones in adolescents.

Every middle school that wants to achieve success must understand the lives of children of parents with biochemical issues. Their parents cannot provide the full amount of support needed for the middle years. When I was a principal, one of my students had a mother with multiple personalities. Her teenage daughter needed help, but only one of the personalities (called Betti) would sign the papers permitting us to provide the help. At our first meeting, the mother came, but not as Betti, so we asked to speak with her. The mother said no; everyone was mad at Betti for getting pregnant. So, the school counselor called the teen's home every day until one morning Betti answered. Knowing Betti was available, the counselor immediately went to the home and had Betti sign the papers. When children live in settings such as this, the necessary supports for developmental growth often are missing because every day is about survival.

Parental addiction also impacts the developmental growth of young adolescents. In the book *Adult Children of Alcoholics* (1990) Woititz identifies several traits that become a part of the psychological makeup of children of alcoholics, for example: secrecy, guessing at what is normal, the need to be perfect, having great difficulty trusting adults, etc. And research shows that when there is an addicted adult in a household, at least one of the children usually becomes an "adult"—a caretaker of the household.

Stress levels are usually quite high in poor households. A Cornell University study found that the allostatic load (the chemical and physiological changes that occur in the body) were elevated for children in poverty. When the allostatic load is high, the body stays in a state of "heightened alert"— i.e., a state of stress—and over time this wears on the body, resulting in illness. When the allostatic load is high, there is less learning because of the impact on brain functioning.

Resiliance

Berger states that resilience is dynamic (may be more resilient at one time than another), is a positive adaptation to stress, and involves significant adversity (2011, p. 353). In fact, Paul Tough (2012) in his research found that even when adolescents had several major challenges and setbacks in their life, nearly all the problems were eliminated by a nurturing caregiver.

Identifying Resources for Psychological Development

When you have a student who is having difficulty with academics or behavior, using this checklist will help you determine the best interventions to make for that particular student. Identify and use the student's present strengths to build strength in the student's less developed areas. Interventions do not work if they are based on what the student does not have. Middle level students can also identify their own resources using this checklist.

Checklist for Identifying Psychological Resources

If a biochemical issue is present, it is addressed with either medication or a series of interventions	Yes	No
Does not use illegal drugs or alcohol	Yes	No
Has at least two friends his/her own age	Yes	No
Has at least one adult on the staff who knows the student	Yes	No
Has at least two adults outside of school who care about the student	Yes	No
Has at least one person he/she admires	Yes	No
Has at least one person he/she admires who is not a sports figure or entertainment celebrity	Yes	No
Can identify the traits he/she admires in a role model	Yes	No
Can identify the kind of person he/she does not want to be	Yes	No
Knows how to make friendships and relationships that are positive and not destructive	Yes	No
Can give and accept compliments	Yes	No
Has access to individuals who have positive and non-destructive success in the dominant culture but have also retained their cultural/racial roots	Yes	No
Knows the history of his/her family or racial/cultural past and examples of successful individuals therein	Yes	No
Has an individual he/she can trust	Yes	No
Has role identity	Yes	No

Source: *Under-Resourced Learners: Eight Strategies to Boost Student Achievement* by R. K. Payne, 2008.

What Interventions Can Help with Psychological Development?

1. Parent training makes a huge difference if the training is about the parent first. My company, aha! Process, has trained 15,000 adults across the United States in a program called Getting Ahead in a Just-Gettin'-By World. This training is mostly about the adult and not his/her children. To develop capacity in others, you must have an understanding of yourself. There is very little conversation in poor households about emotional issues because no one has experience discussing such issues and discussing emotions is considered a sign of weakness.

2. One of the most interesting conversations to have in middle level schools is this: How do you know when someone is a real man? A real woman? What is the value of work and why would anyone want to work?

3. Have students research different careers. In addition, each semester expect them to interview—and record a conversation with—someone very different from them, using a set of questions provided. For example: How did you decide to pursue this career? Is there something you wanted to do instead? How did you learn about this job? What makes you good at your job? What advice would you have for someone who is not sure what to do? Then, in advisory period, discuss the various careers and answers to the questions. How do you know there's another way to think if everyone you know is like you?

4. Make sure every at-risk student (particularly the ones who are going through early puberty and those who have the most discipline referrals) have one adult in the building who talks to them every day, one-on-one, for at least five minutes.

5. All school personnel and definitely all advisors in advisory programs should have training in what support for adolescent developmental issues might be missing at home for children of adults with biochemical issues and how the school will provide support for those children. They need to know what signs to look for in the students' behaviors, etc.

6. Looping, the practice of establishing multiyear arrangements for students and teachers, allows middle grades students to learn to build relationships with adults that form the critical pathways for their learning—education "happens" through relationships. There is abundant evidence that meaningful student to student relationships happen in looping situations that also enhance adolescent development and learning. Multiyear formats result in ongoing, small learning communities where mentoring from older students provides both the older and younger students benefits of increased self-esteem and bonding. Research also shows results of academic and behavioral improvement and increased student engagement in establishing long-term student-teacher relationships. To learn more about looping and the variety of organizational forms it can take, see "Looping and Multiage Grouping: Providing Long-Term Student-Teacher Relationships—and Time" (2013).

7. If you have students with a "victim mentality" use strategies to combat that learned helplessness. There is powerful research showing that students can learn to become their own best advocates. In *Fall Down 7 Times, Get Up 8* (2012), Debbie Silver urges pushing all students to the far reaches of their abilities and giving them the tools to pursue their goals through life's difficult circumstances. Students feel empowered when they learn to focus on things they can control—their effort, perseverance, attitudes, and commitment. She suggests using strategies such as scaffolding, focusing on improvement rather than finite goals, giving task-specific feedback, and helping students overcome setbacks by finding alternative paths to success (pp. 61-64).

SOCIAL-EMOTIONAL DEVELOPMENT

In *This We Believe: Keys to Educating Young Adolescents* (National Middle School Association, 2010), the following characteristics of social-emotional development in young adolescents are listed. (I have rephrased and simplified the original list. For added detail, see *This We Believe*.) The young adolescent:

- Has a strong need for approval and is very concerned about peer acceptance.
- May overreact to minor experiences of embarrassment, ridicule, and rejection.
- Experiences increased harassment because of differences.
- Depends on parents for values and beliefs but wants his/her own as well.
- Benefits from encouragement from adults.
- Enjoy fads.
- Needs peer approval.
- Needs alone time.
- Needs group belonging and may experience alienation from some groups.
- Experiments with slang and "rebellious" behaviors.
- Has mood swings.
- Sometimes demonstrates immaturity in behaviors.

- Shows acceptance of varied maturation rates.
- Begins feeling sexual and romantic attractions.
- Engages in bullying and confrontational experiences.
- Is often socially vulnerable as his or her own identity is being formed.

What Does the Research Indicate About the Social-Emotional Development of Adolescents?

First of all, all emotional well-being is based primarily on two things: safety and belonging. The first place that an individual begins to understand these concepts is in the family or household in which he/she lives.

Bonding and attachment

John Bowlby (1969, 1973, 1980) did research on bonding and attachment and found that there are four principal styles of bonding and attachment.

- The world is a good, safe place.
- The world is a bad, unsafe place.
- I see myself as good.
- I see myself as bad.

Bowlby put young children (6 years old) into a room, one after the other. Each child's primary caregiver was then asked to leave the room. Each child was then observed. Bowlby identified two issues in safety and belonging: connection and exploration. In other words was the child connected enough to the primary caregiver to risk exploration of the room? He identified the following styles of bonding and attachment.

	I see myself as good	*I see myself as bad*
The world is a good, safe place	Secure and attached	Insecure and anxious (scapegoat for the family/group) insecure about worth and value
The world is a bad, unsafe place	Insecure and avoidant (I'm good, but everyone else is bad)	Insecure and unattached (survival of the fittest)

Based on J. Bowlby (1969) Attachment: Attachment and Loss (Vol. 1).

In other words, if I think I am a good person and the world is a safe place, then I am secure and attached. However, if I think I am a bad person, but the world is safe, then I am insecure and anxious. If I see myself as a good person but view the world as a bad place, then I am insecure and avoidant (I will avoid anything or person I think is bad). A person who views himself in the last style believes that he is bad and that the world is unsafe and bad. So it's simply a free-for-all—the survival of the fittest. The research shows part of this last style can come from having a young teen mother who also is insecure.

The research indicates that we bring those styles with us into adulthood—in our romantic relationships, our work relationships, etc. Even though these concepts (views of self and the world) were developed before the age of 6, the understandings play out in adolescence as young people form peer relationships and relationships with adults outside their households. These concepts and perceptions of safety and belonging originate with our families and early caregivers.

Family structure and function

Family structure and family function are often confused. According to Kathleen Berger in *The Developing Person Through the Life Span* (2011), family structure is how the family is configured—e.g., single parent, two parents, mother only, father only, same-sex partners, et al. Family function is how well the family meets the needs of the child in the following areas: basic material needs, learning, self-respect, peer relationships, and harmony and stability (p. 359). If the child is not nurtured and provided the preceding items, the family structure is ineffective.

Family closeness. Very important to emotional well-being is family closeness. Berger (2011, p. 439) defines family closeness in the following four ways:

1. Communication: Do family members talk openly with one another?
2. Support: Do they rely on one another?
3. Connectedness: How emotionally close are they?
4. Control: Do parents encourage or limit adolescent autonomy?

Parental monitoring. One of the things that effective parents do is monitor their children's connections and explorations. Parental knowledge of friends, activities, and schoolwork are key in keeping adolescents on the path to success. In fact, in the research on drug use by students, middle level students had significantly less drug use if the parents knew who the adolescent was with, monitored activities, and didn't use drugs themselves as a way of coping with problems (Parker, 2004).

Other adults. Note that even when the family does not or cannot provide support to the adolescent, another adult relationship that is nurturing and supportive often will stand in the breach. In the research by Tony Bates' Headstrong organization, one strong adult in the life of an adolescent does more to promote the success of that young person than any other variable (Bates, 2012; Dooley & Fitzgerald, 2012). Paul Tough, in his book *How Children Succeed: Grit, Curiosity, and the Hidden Power of Character,* states that, even when a student has excessive difficult personal situations, having a mother or another significant adult who is nurturing to the child mitigates much of the harm that those situations cause.

Peer pressure, peer power, and peer support

While the family unit constitutes the foundation of the middle level student, the student's peers are essential to his or her social development. As they move away from dependence on adults toward independence, their relationships with peers moves "front and center."

According to Oberle and Schonert-Reichl,

> *Decades of research seem to suggest that peer acceptance—the degree to which a child is socially accepted and liked by his or her peers—emerges as a core indicator for social and emotional well-being and academic success during the early adolescent years.* Particularly, studies on peer acceptance during the middle school years indicate that early adolescents who are popular, accepted, and have positive relationships with their peers also tend to be socially well-adjusted, and academically more successful than those who are rejected by their peers. Explanations for the critical role of peer acceptance in academic achievement have centered around the notion that belonging to a friendship group in school can increase motivation to engage in classroom and school activities, and be a valuable source of social support for students in the school context, particularly during early adolescence. (2013, p. 45, emphasis added)

Two key aspects of peer relationships are selection and facilitation. Teens will join a group that has similar values and interests and, in that process of selection, abandon other friends they had previously. After selection comes facilitation of activities, both positive and negative with the new set of friends. "Deviancy training"—in which one person shows another how to rebel against the social norms—can involve teens in actions as part of a group that a teen would not undertake as an individual (Berger, 2011, p. 443).

Romantic interests

This is also the time when early romantic interest begins. Berger writes:

> Dexter Dunphy (1963) identified the sequence of male-female relationships during childhood and adolescence: (1) Groups of friends, exclusively one sex or the other; (2) a loose association of girls and boys, with public interactions within a crowd; (3) small mixed-sex groups of advanced members of the crowd; and (4) formation of couples, with private intimacies. (2011, p. 445)

Research shows that the timing of couple formation is heavily influenced by culture and that forming couples during early adolescence, particularly for girls, is a sign of trouble.

So where do adolescents learn about sex? Often from their peers. In the research, many parents underestimate or are unaware of the activities of their young teens. Teens tend to discuss the details of romance and sex with their peers from whom they seek advice and approval. And they worry that there may be something wrong with them sexually—undersexed, oversexed, deviant, body issues, etc.

Bullying

One aspect of peer interaction, bullying, is significant in young adolescents' social-emotional development. A series of repeated, systematic attacks intended to harm, bullying may be physical, verbal, relational (designed to destroy peer relationships), or cyberbullying. "Victims tend to be 'cautious, sensitive, quiet … lonely and abandoned at school. As a rule they do not have a single good friend in their class' (Olweus, Limber, & Mihalic, 1999, p. 15)" (Berger, 2011, p. 367). Further, girls tend to bully verbally and boys tend to bully physically. Both sexes will use relational and cyberbullying, especially as they get older.

Gender brain differences

Also affecting social emotional development of young adolescents is the difference in processing of the developing brains of males and females. The subsequent information about patterns in gender differences in brain processing, as with all such information, will not "fit" about 6–10% of the population. But since the brain does process in patterns, it's important to note the following:

Males and females generally do not process emotions the same way. Because the corpus callosum on a female is approximately three-fourths of an inch thicker, the communication between the two sides of her brain is quicker. In brain studies, when a female has an emotional "hit," that information suffuses the brain in minutes, and her brain is flooded with estrogen. Her first reaction is to cry and talk. When a male brain has an emotional "hit," it is processed at the base of the skull, and it takes several hours for the information to permeate the brain. The first thing most males will do when they have an emotional "hit" is to get silent, refuse to talk, and ask to be left alone. Furthermore, a male usually doesn't want eye contact when an emotional issue is being discussed. And if males can do an activity with their hands/bodies, they're much more inclined to talk. For example, if I want my son to talk to me, I ask him if we can cook together. Then he talks a lot.

So a female adolescent will want to be with a male and be in conversation with him. The male adolescent will find comfort in the relationship—less for the conversation than for *the presence of the female.* Many early boy-girl conversations are greatly misunderstood on both sides because of the very different gender-based needs and values assigned to romantic relationships.

So, all of the above factors—families; family structures, functions, and closeness; other adults, peers, and gender brain differences—impact the feelings of safety and belonging and thus, the ability of the young adolescent to bond and attach, the social-emotional development of young adolescents.

What Happens to Social-Emotional Development in an Under-Resourced Environment?

Key issues that occur in under-resourced environments include the following: interruptions in bonding/attachment development, abuse, limited family function, survival-of-the-fittest mentality, lack of vocabulary for emotions, lack of positive language, onset of caretaking at a very early age, and "deviancy training" as a reaction to damaging adults.

Research on bonding and attachment shows insecure and unattached children often have a young mother who is insecure herself. Poverty is highly correlated to single-parent households headed by women. Because the teen birth rate is higher among teens in poverty, there's a very high correlation to the children of teen mothers being under-resourced. A study done by Feeding America based on 2009 statistics compiled by the U.S. Department of Agriculture found that in 2010, nearly half (49%) of all the children born in the United States were getting food assistance from WIC, the federal Special Supplemental Nutrition Program for Women, Infants and Children (USDA as cited in Brown, 2011).

Furthermore, **family structure and function tend to be linked to family income.**

> Two factors interfere with family function: low income and high conflict. Many families experience both—because financial stress increases conflict and vice versa (McLanahan, 2009)....If economic hardship is ongoing and parents have little education, that increases stress, making adults tense and hostile toward their partners and children (Conger et al., 2002; Parke et al., 2004). (Berger, 2011, p. 362)

According to Berliner (2009), family stress often leads to family violence. History and experience tell us when the economy is bad and unemployment rises, children do not fare well. From 10–20% of American families have some form of serious family violence annually.

> 50–60% of the women who receive public benefits have experienced physical abuse by an intimate partner at some point during their adult lives. Other data suggest this rate may be as high as 82%....2 out of every 5 Hispanic females in Texas (39%) reported experiencing severe abuse....The number one killer of African American women

between 15 and 34 years old is homicide at the hands of a current or former intimate partner. (Berliner, 2009, pp. 24–25)

Domestic violence makes the parent unavailable to the child emotionally. Children exposed to violence suffer symptoms that resemble post-traumatic stress disorder. In one study with an elementary grade cohort,

> an increase in the number of children from families known to have a history of domestic violence shows a statistically significant correlation to a decrease in the math and reading test scores among the students' peers…. These negative effects were primarily driven by troubled boys acting out. (Berliner, 2009, p. 26)

Numerous factors impinge upon social-emotional development in under-resourced settings. Coupled with family structure and function are neighborhoods and their stress-related data. Berliner's research on urban neighborhoods produced the following results:

- Neighborhood deprivations have a large negative effect on student achievement.
- Neighborhoods can foster violence, crime, and deviant adolescent behavior.
- A Chicago study measured neighborhood responsibility and trust, which are referred to as "collective efficacy." Low collective efficacy accounted for 75% of the variation in violence levels, and low efficacy is associated with violent crime. Research indicates that "high collective efficacy" can be very powerful in keeping poor children on track despite other adverse factors.
- The same Chicago study followed poor children no matter where they moved and rated the neighborhoods. Students were assessed on verbal ability and achievement testing. States Berliner: "The results showed that staying in neighborhoods of concentrated poverty has a cumulative and negative effect on verbal achievement independent of a host of other factors."
- Neighborhood effects rival family effects in influencing child development. (Berliner. 2009)

Given the realities of under-resourced neighborhoods, often the safest place for children is at school.

Poverty fosters bullying

Neighborhoods of high poverty frequently generate physical bullies because bullying is a survival method in a win-lose environment. Often students join gangs because it's a way to stay safer and have at least some protection. If you do not join a gang, you are often beaten up by all the gangs. In other words, you have no protection.

Paul Tough (2012) has described a study of how trauma impacts the risks for young adolescents called ACE. He writes that in the ACE (Adverse Childhood Experiences) study, participants scored 1 point for each trauma suffered in ten categories of adverse childhood experiences: physical and sexual abuse, physical and emotional neglect, household dysfunction (incarceration, mental illness, addiction), etc. The results were

- With a score of 4 or higher, adolescents were twice as likely to smoke, were seven times more likely to be alcoholics, and were more likely to have sex before age 15. Also, 51% with a score of 4 or higher had learning or behavioral problems.
- With a score of 0, only 3% of adolescents had learning or behavioral problems.

Tough concludes that the most effective antidote to adverse situations was

> Parents and other caregivers who are able to form close, nurturing relationships with their children can foster resilience in them that protects them from many of the worst effects of a harsh early environment.... The effect is biochemical." (Tough, 2012)

In the field of science right now, no one knows how relationships change experience from a biochemical point of view.

Identifying Emotional Resources

When you have a student who is having difficulty with academics or behavior, using this checklist will help you determine the best interventions to make for that particular student. Identify and use the student's present strengths to build strength in the student's less developed areas. Interventions do not work if they are based on what the student does not have. Middle level students can also identify their own resources using this checklist.

Checklist for Identifying Emotional Resources

Controls impulsivity most of the time	Yes	No
Can plan for behavior to complete assignments	Yes	No
Controls anger	Yes	No
Has positive self-talk	Yes	No
Sees the relationship between choice and consequence	Yes	No
Can usually resolve a problem with words (does not hit or become verbally abusive)	Yes	No
Can argue without vulgarity or profanity	Yes	No
Can predict outcomes based on cause and effect	Yes	No
Can separate the behavior (criticism) from the person (contempt)	Yes	No
Usually has the words to name feelings	Yes	No
Can use the adult voice	Yes	No
Has parents who are supportive of school	Yes	No
Has at least two adults who care about and nurture him/her	Yes	No
Has at least two friends (peers) who are nurturing and not destructive	Yes	No
Belongs to a peer group; can be racial, cultural, religious, activity-based (e.g., sports, music, academics), etc.	Yes	No
Is involved in one or more school activities (sports, music, theater, chess club, etc.)	Yes	No
Is good at making new friends (social capital)	Yes	No
Has at least two friends who are different from him/her (by race, culture, interest, academics, religion, etc.)	Yes	No
Is a mentor or a friend to whom others come for advice	Yes	No
Has at least two people who will advocate for him/her	Yes	No
Is connected to a larger social network (bridging social capital—e.g., church, 4-H, Boys and Girls Club, soccer league, country club, etc.)	Yes	No
Can identify at least one group to which he/she belongs	Yes	No
Has at least one teacher or coach who knows him/her personally and will advocate for him/her	Yes	No
Has at least one adult who is the primary support system for the household	Yes	No

Source: *Under-Resourced Learners: Eight Strategies to Boost Student Achievement* by R. K. Payne, 2008.

What Interventions Can Help with Social-Emotional Development?

Using the process indicated in the following chart can help to guide both students and parents through "normal" emotional issues. If a problem involves mental illness, a biochemical issue, or trauma (abuse, profound neglect, etc.), then it needs to be referred to a licensed professional.

Questions to Help Parents and Students Address Emotional Issues

STEP	QUESTIONS FOR STUDENTS	QUESTIONS FOR PARENTS
1 PROBLEM	What happened? What is bothering you?	What do you know about what happened? What is your understanding?
2 SAFETY/BONDING	What about this makes you feel unsafe? Who cares the most about you? Whom do you care the most about?	Are you concerned for the safety of your child? Can you name an adult at the school that you feel cares about your child?
3 FEARS (usually behind anger is fear)	What is the worst thing that could happen? On a scale of 1–10 (10 being a high level of energy), how much energy are you giving it?	What is the worst thing that could happen? What are the "what if" questions you are asking yourself?
4 SATIATION	When this kind of thing happens, what do you do to feel better about it? (Talk to a friend, get high, quit working …?)	If you were king or queen of the world, how would you address or "fix" this? What would make you feel better as a parent in this situation?
5 PERSONAL CONTRIBUTION	What did you do to make the situation better or worse?	In this situation as a parent, do you feel you helped your child more or hurt your child more? To what extent did or did not your child act on your advice? Have you had similar reactions?

6 WHAT WAS LOST?	What about this situation makes you feel "less than"? Has this kind of situation happened before?	Do you believe that this situation is a reflection on your parenting? What do you think your child has "lost" in this experience?
7 ACCEPTANCE	What is the reality—brutal facts—about what happened? Do you resent the consequences?	What must we accept in this situation? Did your child "lose" anything as a result of this situation? Do you think the consequences will result in a change in behavior?
8 VALIDATING EXPERIENCES	Tell me about a time when you were successful in dealing with a situation like this. Tell me about any situation in which you think you do really well.	Tell me about the situations and areas in which your child does well.
9 RECLAIMING SELF	What about that successful experience could we use in this situation? What are other choices that could be used to "win" in this situation more often?	How will we help your child be more successful—i.e., win more often—in this type of situation?
10 CHANGE, MOMENTUM, ACCOUNTABILITY, PRACTICE	What will you do next time? What cues you to do what you did? How can you change that cue? How will you practice that?	How will you support your child in this situation?

Source: *How Much of Yourself Do You Own? A Handbook for Developing Emotional Resources* by R. K. Payne, in press

Another way to build in better social-emotional development is to have every child (if possible) participate in extracurricular activities and to make sure the following things happen at school:

1. Ensure every student has someone to eat with every day; never let students eat alone.

2. Provide classroom activities in which students work in pairs on an academic task. Talking opens neural pathways, and it's a "forced socialization." The current research on adolescent males is that large numbers of them have fewer verbal/emotional skills because of the amount of time they're in front of a computer screen (video gaming, porn, etc.) (Zimbardo & Duncan, 2012).

3. Give each new student an "ambassador," another student who accompanies the new student for two to three days (eats lunch with him/her, shows the new student where his/her classes are, etc.). This lowers the amount of activity in deviancy training and allows the neophytes to be introduced and meet people.

4. Address bullying. In the organizational research, there is a term "isomorphism"—i.e., what happens at one level of the organization happens at all levels of the organization. So if there is cheating that goes unchecked at the bottom of a company, there is almost sure to be cheating at the top of the company. Likewise, the research on effective curtailment of bullying is the following: "Everyone in the school must change, not just the identified bullies; intervention is more effective in the earlier grades, and evaluation is critical; programs that appear to be good might actually be harmful" (Berger, 2011, p. 368).

5. Help friends be better friends; this is another wonderful intervention. One counselor did the following at a secondary school. Each student was asked to identify his/her five best friends. Then the students identified the kinds of topics they discussed with their friends (students did not identify themselves). The counselor found that students generally identified best friends by clique or group. What the school did was to tally who the best friends were in each grade. Then they had three- to

four-hour meetings in which the best friends were taught to be even better friends—and also when to refer a situation to an adult because it was dangerous for the student (suicide, violence, bullying, etc.). In essence, the school built another layer of safety and belonging into the school.

6. Teach students and adults how to stay out of the "Karpman triangle" (Karpman, 1968). Particularly in situations where losses have been linked to abuse (for example: "I will let my partner sexually violate you so that I can have a place to live") and boundaries are either very rigid or non-existent. Part of taking responsibility for your value is learning to say no. Part of establishing boundaries and saying no is to avoid the Karpman triangle. Establishing boundaries is rarely possible when one is in the triangle.

Karpman Triangle

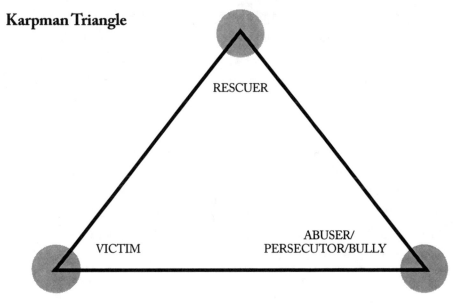

RESCUER

VICTIM

ABUSER/
PERSECUTOR/BULLY

Source: Karpman, S. (1968). Fairy tales and script drama analysis. *Transactional Analysis Bulletin, 7*(26), 39–43.

One person can perform each of the three roles. In one setting the person is a bully, in another setting the person is a rescuer, and in another setting the person is a victim. Once you are in the triangle, you will eventually take on all three roles. To avoid and stay out of the triangle, you can ask questions. ***Please note: When we get in the triangle, boundaries disappear. The problem can never be solved if you stay in the triangle.***

For example, when my son was 8 years old, he came home from school and told me that he was bored in school. He presented himself as a victim and asked me to go to school and "rescue" him by "bullying" the teacher. So I asked him whose problem it was that he was bored. He said it was the teacher's problem. So I asked him, "Is the teacher bored?" He said, "No, I am." So I said, "It isn't the teacher's problem. It's your problem. Since it's your problem, how can you solve it?" Then we talked about what he could do to not be bored at school. By asking questions, I stayed out of the triangle (Payne, in press).

If I had gotten into the triangle with him, then I would have gone to school to bully the teacher so that I could rescue my son who was a victim. The teacher would have then felt like a victim so she would have gone to her principal to be rescued by calling me the parent in and bullying me. I, as the parent, would have felt like a victim; I would have gone home to my husband and told him, so that he would rescue me by going to school and bullying the principal. Then the principal would have felt like a victim and he would have gone to his superintendent…. And it never stops.

7. As parent training, provide newsletters and DVDs about the stages students go through as adolescents and what they can expect. Most parents know very little about the stages of adolescent development. The more the parent knows, the better it is for the student.

8. Interview each student and ask him/her these two questions: Who cares the most about you? Who do you care the most about? If the student does not mention an adult, then find a staff member (teacher, custodian, bus driver, etc.) who is willing to talk to that student one-on-one each day for 3–5 minutes. They can just check in with questions such as: How are you doing? Did you have enough to eat? And so on. This one intervention makes a huge difference in achievement and discipline.

WHAT SCHOOLS CAN DO TO IMPROVE THE SUCCESS AND ACHIEVEMENT OF STUDENTS IN POVERTY

Before getting into the details of what schools can do to improve the success and achievement of under-resourced students, let's take a look at the bigger picture regarding those schools. I find the following 2011 analysis from Hopson and Lee helpful as we start this discussion.

> A persistent achievement gap continues to place students from poor families at dispro-portionately high risk for dropout. The dropout rate among these students is 10 times the rate among students from higher-income families. They experience higher rates of problem behavior in school and academic difficulty. Specifically, students who partici-pate in the free- and reduced-price lunch program are likely to perform poorly in read-ing and math, receive low scores on standardized tests, and report low overall GPA. ...

> The research literature provides evidence that social supports for students can moder-ate the impact of poverty and its associated stressors. Increasingly, research points to characteristics of the school environment as critical for learning and healthy devel-opment. School climates characterized by supportive relationships, emotional and physical safety, and shared goals for learning are associated with school connectedness and academic success.

> ... A positive climate seems to have the strongest positive impact on student outcomes in high poverty schools. Schools with large numbers of students from poor families are most successful in meeting learning objectives when they have school climates characterized by collegiality, collaboration, shared decision-making, positive attitudes, high quality instruction, and a clear mission. The severity of educational problems

commonly found in urban, minority schools are reduced by a cohesive social context. A positive school climate also predicts better social skills and school adjustment.

Among students with the most positive perceptions of the school climate, there was no significant difference in the behavior of students from poor or higher income families. The effect was similar for both boys and girls. (p. 2221)

How Do You Produce a Positive School Climate?

If Hopson and Lee (2011) are correct regarding the importance of a positive school climate, the question becomes: How is a positive school climate achieved? I believe that a positive school climate is a lot like classroom management. To be successful, both require structures in place that allow for a smooth daily operation, regardless of crisis. Discussions about school climate often center on relationships but not the underlying structures that allow those relationships to flourish. I see 13 keys to establishing and maintaining a positive school climate. Here's my baker's dozen:

- Leadership
- Relationships of mutual respect between and among students and educators
- Deeply embedded processes and structures
- Cultural and institutional diversity
- Emphasis on the rigor of student work and performance
- Collegial working relationships between and among teachers and staff
- Students with future stories
- District level support for middle level staff development
- District level support for advisory periods
- District level support for extracurricular activities
- District level development of expertise in administrators and teachers
- District level support for parent training that builds the capacity of the parent as an individual
- Community involvement

Leadership

The first issue in establishing a positive school climate is leadership. I am very concerned about the de-emphasis in the last ten years on the impact that principals and district and system level leaders have on the outcomes of their schools. The focus has been on teachers, and training for administrators has become technical—i.e., how to evaluate the teacher, how to assess data, how to work with parents.

But the real issue in attaining a positive school climate is LEADERSHIP. Leadership includes conflict resolution, political assessments of feasible realities, teacher development, student analysis, developing expertise as a leader, decision making, protecting the parameters of learning, etc. In the wonderful book *A Failure of Nerve: Leadership in the Age of the Quick Fix* (2007) Edwin H. Friedman argues persuasively that what changes organizations, families, and churches is primarily leadership by an individual.

Friedman identifies three characteristics of "deadlocked" systems: "(1) an unending treadmill of trying harder; (2) looking for answers rather than reframing questions; and (3) either/or thinking that creates false dichotomies" (p. 34). Furthermore, Friedman identifies

> the problem of contemporary America's orientation toward leadership as: (1) a regressive, counter-evolutionary trend in which the most dependent members of any organization set the agendas and where the adaption is constantly toward weakness rather than strength, (2) a devaluation of the process of individuation so that leaders tend to rely more on expertise than on their own capacity to be decisive, (3) an obsession with data and technique that has become a form of addiction and turns professionals into data-junkies and their information into data junkyards, and (4) a widespread misunderstanding about the relational nature of destructive processes in families and institutions … (p. 12)

He goes on to say that the data junkyards do the following to leadership: "overwhelm leaders, confuse them with contradictory results, emphasize weakness rather than strength, and de-self them by ignoring the variable of individuation" (p. 98).

In short, what Friedman is saying is that leaders ignore the human realities of the situation, constantly seek "data" to defend themselves and their position, and in effect, abdicate the very leadership they are charged with implementing.

In the many years I have been working in schools, when I see a very successful, high-achieving school, I *always* see a strong, decisive leader. *Always*.

A strong leader does these things: guards the parameters (i.e., does not let the well-being of children be hijacked by individuals, institutional quirks, time stealers, misguided research, or political whims); is inclusive of parents and students; sets the standards for behavior for both students and adults; and maintains high expectations and high support.

Relationships of mutual respect

Relationships of mutual respect between and among students and educators are the foundation of all learning. All learning is double coded—emotionally and cognitively (Greenspan & Benderly, 1997). Mutual respect means that there are high expectations (you *will* learn this), high levels of support (we will help you with this), and insistence (I insist on it). There is a deep understanding and accommodation of individual needs, while at the same time, there is unwavering insistence, support, and high expectations.

Deeply embedded processes and structures

It isn't possible to have a strong supportive culture without processes and structures to make that happen. These include such things as a systematic method of keeping track of the well-being and learning of each student, emotional support systems (advisory period—more on that later), support systems for teachers, a process for consistently engaging parents and involving the community, and a process for involving all students in extracurricular activities. These processes and structures ensure the well-being of each student despite the (almost daily) crises that inevitably occur.

Hidden rules

All races, ethnic groups, regions of the country, religions, social classes, and institutions have "hidden rules." These rules are followed but are very seldom articulated. Group members follow them and judge negatively those individuals who don't follow the hidden rules. Often one's knowledge—or lack of knowledge—about hidden rules is equated with intelligence.

To survive school and work, your students need to know the hidden rules of school and work. For the hidden rules of poverty, see my book, *A Framework for Understanding Poverty: A Cognitive Approach* (Payne, 2013).

Resources for Assessing Knowledge of Hidden Rules

When a student is having academic or behavioral issues, both the teacher and the student can use this checklist to assess the student's familiarity with the school's hidden rules. Using this process will help you determine the most effective interventions for that particular student. Identify and use the student's present strengths to build strength in the his or her less developed areas. Interventions do not work if they are based on what the student does not have.

Checklist for Assessing Knowledge of Hidden Rules

Can identify and avoid the "pet peeves" of the person in charge, i.e., boss, teacher, et al.	Yes	No
Can identify at school or work what will actually get you into trouble versus what the rules say will get you into trouble	Yes	No
Is successful with different teachers, students, and bosses	Yes	No
Can work/learn from someone even if he/she does not like that person	Yes	No
Can assess a situation and determine which behaviors can be used and which ones cannot in order to be successful in that situation	Yes	No
Can articulate what the hidden rules are in a given situation or with a given person	Yes	No
Can differentiate between the "real" authority and the stated authority in a given situation	Yes	No
Knows the hidden rules of the school environment	Yes	No
Knows the hidden rules of the work environment	Yes	No
Can assess the unspoken cueing mechanisms in a given situation or with a given person and use that information to his/her advantage	Yes	No

Source: *Under-Resourced Learners: 8 Strategies to Boost Student Achievement* (p. 13), by R. K. Payne, 2009.

One of the things that successful schools do is make sure these "rules" are articulated and taught so that all students can be successful. I've done this by asking students if they use the same rules in basketball that they do in football. When they respond no, I ask them, "Why not?" They immediately understand that they would lose the game, and are engaged in identifying the hidden rules for becoming successful in school and life.

Rigor of student work and performance

The success and achievement of under-resourced students depends on educators who emphasize rigor in students' work and performance—the same questions are asked about their work as are asked about other students' work: Are the assignments tied to the standards? Are the assignments rigorous and interesting? Or is it "Answer the questions at the end of the chapter"?

One of the developments in the last 10 years of education is to scrutinize the teacher (the state of Georgia has a 24-page teacher evaluation instrument) but to pay virtually no attention to student work or the calibration of that work. What is calibration? It's when the assignment is matched with the rigor of the standards at that grade level.

Not long ago I was in a sixth-grade classroom of a low-performing middle school. As in many classrooms, the standard for the day's emphasis was posted on the board: to "identify character development in literature." Students were coloring in a coloring book. When asked about the rationale for this assignment, the teacher explained that the students could not read. Although there are many ways to teach character development without reading, she didn't know any of those ways.

Content-specific expertise must be used to build rigor into assignments. For example, what follows is a rubric to develop a skilled musician. I wrote this with an orchestra teacher who wanted to develop expertise in his students rather than proficiencies.

Skilled Musician Rubric (for band and orchestra members)

CRITERIA	1	2	3	4
Accuracy	Not in correct time Several wrong notes Wrong key	Mostly in correct time Misses notes Key is correct Fingerings are off	In correct time Mostly uses correct fingerings Notes are correct	Timing is virtually always correct Fingerings are correct Notes are virtually always correct
Articulation	No variation in tempo Markings not observed No contrast in sound	Some variation in tempo but not correct Some contrast but incorrect for piece Random use of markings	Tempo mostly correct Mostly correct use of markings Dynamic contrast thin but correct	Markings are virtually always observed and followed Wide range of dynamic contrast Tempo is correct
Sound quality	Thin timbre High and low notes off Too loud or too soft for note or section Unpleasant to ear	Timbre for most notes is fuller All difficult notes have some timbre Use of sound markings is random	Timbre is mostly full Sound markings are used but not advantageously	Timbre is full Sound markings are correctly interpreted and followed
Interpretation	No meaning assigned to piece No understanding of intent or purpose of composer	Playing indicates emotion but little understanding of meaning Understands that piece has climax but does not know where it is	Playing mostly conveys meaning and always conveys emotion Understands role of climax Can talk about intent and purpose	Playing conveys meaning and emotion Climax can be identified Plays truly to intent and purpose

continued

Skilled Musician Rubric (for band and orchestra members) *continued*

Ensemble contribution	Does not pay attention to conductor Listens only to his/her playing Too loud/too soft for group	Periodically pays attention to conductor Is mostly in balance with group Listens to his/her section Little understanding of his/her contribution to melody	Mostly follows conductor's interpretations Is in balance with group as whole Mostly listens to piece as whole Can verbally articulate contribution to melody but does not always reflect that in his/her playing	Follows conductor's interpretation Is in balance with group Listens to piece as whole Understands his/her contribution to melody

Source: *Developing Expertise and Rigor* by R. K. Payne, 2013.

After students played a piece, they used a highlighter on the rubric to assess their performance. Then, using a different-colored highlighter, the teacher assessed the performance. The student then made a plan for addressing any discrepancies. For tools and examples of how to do this, see my book *Building Student Expertise and Rubrics* (scheduled for publication in early 2014).

Every student has a future story

One of the requirements for every student in middle school should be a "future story," which is a realistic plan for what he/she will do in the future. Having such a future story is absolutely crucial for long-term success. Students can use the following form to develop their own future stories.

FUTURE STORY NAME:
You are 10 years older than you are now. You are the star of a movie. What are you doing? Who is with you? Circle any of these that are in your future story: children; job; career; marriage/partnership; health; wealth; travel; living in a city, town, or rural area; living in another country; vehicles; hobbies; sports; music; movies; college, technical school, military service; church/religion; Internet; video games; friends; family; other.
For which of these reasons do you want to graduate from high school? To keep track of money; to know I am getting paid correctly; to go on to college, technical school, or the military; to get a better job; to take care of my parents and/or siblings; to afford my hobbies; to pay for my vehicle; to take care of my children; other.
What do you enjoy doing and would do even if you did not get paid for it? What do you need to do so you can do that and get paid for doing it?
Who are the friends and adults who will help you achieve your future story?
Write out your future story and include how education will help you achieve it.   Signature: Date:

Source: *Research-Based Strategies: Narrowing the Achievement Gap for Under-Resourced Students* by R. K. Payne (2009).

When a student cannot imagine a future story, I ask him/her, "What would you do even if you did not get paid for it, simply because you love to do it?" If the student has a totally unrealistic future story (for example, they want to be an NFL player, but they are not involved in sports), then I give them data and information. For example: 5 years after leaving the NFL, 67% are bankrupt, they lose an average 2-3 inches in height, play an average of 3 years before they are injured or out, and pay 50% of their money in taxes. Then I ask if the student might like to consider a second play—a backup plan.

Support for advisory

Another way the district can help all middle grades students achieve success is to provide support for advisory periods. The position paper of the Association for Middle Level Education, *This We Believe: Keys to Educating Young Adolescents* (NMSA, 2010), states that meeting the affective needs of young adolescents markedly increases their academic success and personal growth.

> Therefore, every adult in developmentally responsive middle level schools serves as an advocate, advisor, and mentor. The concept of advocacy is fundamental to the school's culture, embedded in its every aspect. Advocacy is not a singular event or a period in the schedule; it is an attitude of caring that translates into actions, big and small, when adults respond to the needs of each young adolescent in their charge. (p. 35)

The paper later recommends, "Each student must have one adult in the school who assumes special responsibility for supporting that student's academic and personal development" (p. 35).

Sometimes advisory periods are cut from the schedule (other than money) because they are poorly structured and ineffective. A district can support advisory by (a) providing a good, solid curriculum and approach to middle level advisory periods; (b) providing the training to support it; and (c) evaluating and analyzing student feedback consistently, then adapting the approach to meet the needs.

In "Advocacy Through Advisory" (2013), Philip Brown lists some of the potential purposes of advisory programs.

- To ensure every student becomes well known by one adult in the school
- To ensure that students have an opportunity to know one another and develop new friendships
- To assist in the social/emotional development of young adolescents
- To assist students with academic and learning problems and to monitor their academic progress
- To help students identify their interests and aptitudes and initiate career planning
- To give students a voice as participants in a democratic learning community
- To increase communication and involvement of parents and families
- To promote a safe school environment
- To promote service-learning and community involvement (p. 578)

Advisory periods are particularly beneficial in addressing the needs of under-resourced learners if they are focused on the learner and what can be done to move the learner forward. "There is substantial evidence showing advisory's positive impact in meeting affective and behavioral goals" (Brown, p. 583).

Service-Learning and extracurricular opportunities

Research shows that students are more engaged in academics when they perceive their learning is for a real purpose and that students who get involved with community issues while learning the required curriculum are more likely to engage in their communities as adults (Thompson, 2013). If the service-learning projects are a balance of acquiring academic knowledge and skills and providing service to the community, students have experience and practice in approaching community problems with an open mind and collaborative spirit; appreciating different perspectives; and analyzing data and making decisions based on information they have gathered.

Research shows benefits of students participating in high-quality service-learning to be higher levels of engagement, increased feelings of educational accomplishment, higher rates of homework achievement, positive impact on personal and interpersonal development, and higher levels of achievement. In addition, research shows that students who struggle academically are especially responsive to service-learning programs (Thompson pp. 251–258).

Extracurricular activities, too, are important for the full development of young adolescents' capacities. In order to have full involvement and engagement of the students, it's essential that each student be able to participate in an extracurricular activity. Because of the costs of such efforts, district level support is imperative.

Middle level professional development

Research shows that specialized middle grades preparation programs have essential components of history and philosophy of middle school education; young adolescent development; middle grades organization and curriculum; subject matter knowledge; middle school planning, teaching, and assessment; advocacy for young adolescents and their schools; middle school field experiences; middle grades faculty; and social justice. An encouraging trend is for the adoption of national standards for middle school teacher preparation for some states' own required state teacher preparation and licensure standards. However, in numerous states, middle grades teacher preparation and licensure remain low priorities McEwin & Smith (2013).

It's often the reality that middle level teachers in a district have a mix of elementary and secondary certification, and there may be little understanding of adolescents in the 10- to15-year-old age range. It is vital that professional development be provided by the district for teachers to understand this particular age range and level.

Content for professional development. In many districts, when a new superintendent arrives or a new principal comes aboard, he or she discards whatever previous staff development programs were in place. The new leader starts new initiatives, and continuity and progress are halted in light of the "flavor of the year." Principals frequently have few vehicles to offer support to one or two new staff persons, to review previous training that isn't fully embedded, or to meet the specific needs of their campus. Combined with budget realities, educating staff about the developmental needs of middle schoolers is a real challenge. Fortunately, an abundance of resources are available for customizing professional development to suit your particular school (and its budget) and faculty. "All" it takes is some hard work, listening skills, ability to inspire the faculty, and leadership in collaboration.

District, campus, individual PD. When I was Director of Professional Development for a school district of 18,000 students, one of the things I did was to build, with the principals, a comprehensive staff development approach using the following grid. The principals identified needs at the three levels—district programs, individual campus initiatives, and individual staff needs. The needs tended to be the same from campus to campus by level. For example, the district had initiated a new reading program at the elementary level and an offering was repeated several times at different elementary schools. So, that was listed under "District" and "instructional." If a principal was hiring a new teacher for the next year and wanted them to have that training, it was listed under "instructional" at the individual level. Even though it had been completed at the district level, it was repeated every year at the individual level so that new teachers could be trained. It's important to offer a strong platform of ongoing support and implementation and not get caught up in offering something new each year.

Another consistent offering resulted from several principals reporting their staff members were having difficulty with discipline techniques and classroom management. When I was Director of Staff Development, all the middle school principals came to me and said that they wanted to do a full day of staff development on middle level issues. I worked with them to identify who the experts were that they wanted to learn from, and we provided them with the very focused, intense experience they chose.

Staff Development Content

	COMMUNITY	LEADERSHIP	INSTRUCTIONAL	SUPPORT STAFF
District Mandates				
Campus Needs				
Individual Staff Needs				

Development of expertise

Successful academic performance for under-resourced students is dependent upon district level development of expertise in administrators and teachers. Currently, most of our administrator and teacher evaluations are built upon proficiencies—not expertise. Expertise is the ability to know your own discipline (content) and marry it to the world outside of that content for innovation and effectiveness. We have often used rubrics to identify graduated performance on a task but not on the *development of the person as an expert*. What follows are two rubrics I've used to help identify and evaluate expert principals and teachers.

To use this, principals first rate themselves using one color highlighter, then the supervisor uses a different color of highlighter to assess the principal. Then they discuss the differences in assessment and form a plan that will be used to enhance the performance of the principal. In the same way, the principal and teacher assess the teacher's performance using the Expert Teacher Rubric that follows.

Expert Secondary Principal

	BEGINNING	DEVELOPING	CAPABLE	EXPERT
Safe and culturally competent learning environment	Arbitrary discipline. Little analysis by race or class or gender of building patterns. Unsafe physical and verbal environment.	Discipline tends to be punitive rather than instructive. Focus is on individual student rather than overall structures, patterns, approaches. Individuals are not confronted (80% of referrals come from 11% of staff and 90% of referrals come from 10% of students). Staff bullies students.	Structures safe environment and monitors safety—verbally, physically, and emotionally. Cultural competencies are evident. Students and staff feel safe. Discipline interactions are designed to be instructive and supportive rather than punitive.	Very safe and calm environment. Inclusive and relational by intent and design. Sexism, racism, bullying, etc., are not tolerated. Students are involved in creating the safety. Multiple monitors are developed to enhance well-being.
Operations (budgets, buildings, staff, central office relationships)	Facility poorly maintained and repaired. Dirty. Budget is messy. Not exactly sure of how many staff or students. Few procedures for anything. Frequently badmouths and blames central office.	Building somewhat clean. Makes budget mistakes but uses budget according to guidelines. Tolerates central office. Often tardy with written reports. Follows district procedures and policies most of time.	Follows and uses budget for student well-being. Reports are on time. Relationships with central office are mostly congenial. Building is clean. Repairs are made. Follows district policies.	Skilled and innovative with budget to meet student/staff needs. Building well-kept. Staff organization is excellent, procedures outlined, roles defined, communication smooth and timely. Develops relationships with central office to enhance campus operations.

continued

	BEGINNING	DEVELOPING	CAPABLE	EXPERT
Student achievement	Pays little attention to it. Focuses on daily crises. Does not participate in developing schedule. Few positive interactions with students. Blames students or parents.	Interacts with students. Knows problem ones and "heroes." Little understanding of student achievement. Makes arbitrary decisions during teacher evaluation about students. Very little understanding of learning.	Knows half of students by name. Is in halls. Talks to students; asks about their courses. Has data on course and class achievement. Meets with departments to identify ways in which he/she can provide support for greater student achievement.	Clarifies and maintains role of protector of high student performance. Structures schedule, department performance and counselors to enhance student achievement. Keenly aware of student data.
Staff performance	Few expectations for staff. Faculty bullies run building. Wants loyalty more than performance. Very little interest in instruction.	Knows most staff by name. Staff meetings focus on students and instruction—not operations. Can confront individual staff members. Uses walk-throughs to monitor staff.	Focuses staff performance using data and student work. Structures PLCs (professional learning communities) to focus on student performance. Monitors department performance as it relates to student achievement. Seeks professional development for staff.	Holds staff to high expectations. Provides support so those goals can be reached. Teacher expertise developed. No tolerance for underperformance of staff. Provides excellent staff development.

continued

Expert Secondary Principal *(continued)*

	BEGINNING	DEVELOPING	CAPABLE	EXPERT
Community/ parent outreach and communication	Parents are not welcome. Web page limited. Does not have positive image in community.	Limited communication and involvement with parents and community PR. Sees campus as separate from community.	Sees campus as integral part of community. Regularly seeks opinion outside of campus. Uses multiple communication mechanisms. Does not necessarily seek positive PR.	Builds deep network of relationships outside campus. Structures and encourages parent involvement via DVDs, Web, e-mail, paper, etc. Sees parents as vital to school community. Seeks positive PR for building.
Conflict resolution and management skills	Needs to be liked. Poor or no decisions. Blames others. No integrity of word. May exacerbate conflict.	Procrastinates or uses win/ lose approach. Unpredictable responses. Gathers only part of data. Has difficulty separating person from issue.	Uses a win–win approach. Does not participate in triangulation. Keeps his/ her word. Needs to be respected. Focuses on issue rather than person.	Identifies boundaries of decision (finds BATNA: best alternative to negotiated agreement). Has high integrity. Makes decisions in terms of well-being of students. Builds climate of participation and mutual respect. Focuses on win–win.
Students, sports, extracurricular activities	Focuses on favorite sport or activity. Little attention to big picture or participation.	Tries to be unbiased in support. Does not focus much on equitable participation by gender, race, or talent.	Overtly seeks participation and involvement. Knows results of activities. Attends when possible. Emphasizes academics, as well as sports.	Makes sure almost every student participates. Makes sure all activities are sponsored and supported. Involves students in development.

Source: *Developing Expertise and Rigor* by R. K. Payne, 2013.

	BEGINNING	DEVELOPING	CAPABLE	EXPERT
Safe, culturally competent learning environment	Little classroom management. No clear procedures. Has favorite students and ignores others. Engages in negative comments about students during class. Many discipline referrals. May blur physical or verbal boundaries.	Classroom is usually calm, with procedures and discipline established. Some relational aggression between students. Cultural differences not always understood. Helps students when requested. Boundaries are generally appropriate and intact.	Establishes mutual respect in classroom (support, insistence, high expectations). Calm, businesslike atmosphere. Classroom is relational and inclusive. Actively ensures student well-being.	Rapport with nearly every student. Positive regard for competency, culture, and individuality of each student. Gets best from students. Students have great respect for teacher. Addresses emotional issues appropriately.
Student achievement	Gives formative assessments but doesn't use results for decision making in instruction. May blame students for not learning. Assignments often not on grade level. Doesn't know value of relationships in learning. Doesn't know names of many of his/her students.	Gives feedback and correctives on student work. Most assignments on grade level. Has relationships of respect with some students. May work with individual students to augment their instructional needs. Slow to pick up on needs of highly mobile students. Knows most students' names.	Knows where he/she wants each student to be by end of year. Can discuss each student with some accuracy by name and achievement characteristics. Welcomes questions from students and quickly assesses new students for achievement levels. Most students are in top two quartiles.	By end of first month of school, has accurate assessment of individual achievement needs of each student. Daily tailors group and individual instruction to get phenomenal growth from each student. Takes students to new levels of competence and promotes their growth.

continued

Expert Teacher Rubric *(continued)*

	BEGINNING	DEVELOPING	CAPABLE	EXPERT
Content expertise (purpose, structure, patterns, processes)	Limited understanding of content. Can seldom sort important from unimportant.	Heavily dependent on textbooks, curriculum assists, etc. Unable to clearly explain content and translate to students' understandings.	Good understanding of content. Clearly explains it with stories, examples, drawings, mental models. Processes are clearly taught. Knows when students are confused versus totally wrong.	Extraordinary understanding of content. Frames it so students can understand quickly. Teaches both conceptually and in great detail. Students often develop additional interest in content outside of class.
Student intervention and diagnosis	Says, "I treat them all the same." Makes few adjustments for individual students. Unable to assess what would work with individual students. Many failures.	Interventions used but not necessarily successful. Accuracy of student performance limited. Often will say, "I don't know what to do." Tends to be surprised by student failures.	Quick, accurate intervention and diagnosis. Doesn't wait for students to fail. Will seek support for students from multiple sources. Some failures.	Often uses preventive interventions before students can falter or become discouraged. Almost always intervenes accurately. Few failures.

continued

	BEGINNING	DEVELOPING	CAPABLE	EXPERT
Teaching performance	Lots of "busy work." Instruction disconnected. Much what instruction but very little how and why. Teaching is done "to" students, not "with" them.	Instructional design is solid but fails to engage many students. Pedagogy is limited. Gaps in explanation. Little why in instruction. Has difficulty monitoring group and individuals. Tends to get sidetracked.	Lesson is connected to most students' interests. Varied pedagogy. Opportunity to question and interact with teacher. Teacher monitors both group as a whole and individuals within group simultaneously.	There's flow to instruction (regardless of pedagogy) —seamless, almost effortless, but exceedingly effective. Individually and collectively, students are engaged. Relaxed, yet intense, approach to learning. Students leave wanting to know more. Humor is often part of instruction.
Paperwork, organizational and legal responsibilities, professional ethics	Misses deadlines frequently. Not cognizant of legal implications of decisions. Often must be prompted about paperwork. Grading procedures, standards compliance, etc., are questionable. Often creates difficulties with other staff and administration.	Meets most deadlines. Is aware of most legal implications and responds appropriately. Grades and other paperwork are accurate. Tolerated but not necessarily respected by other staff.	Paperwork and organization are good. Grades are accurate and careful. Responsibilities, including legal, are addressed. Professional ethics are invariably present. Is generally respected by other staff.	Paperwork completed. Virtually always organized and legal. Highly respected by other staff members, even if they don't agree. Grades are respected. Works to create better staff relationships. Asset to campus and community.

continued

Expert Teacher Rubric *(continued)*

	BEGINNING	DEVELOPING	CAPABLE	EXPERT
Parental contact and interaction	Blames parents or avoids parents. Little predictable communication with them. Often condescending to or defensive with parents during conferences.	Contacts parents if there is difficulty with student. Other communication with parents is limited. In conferencing, lectures more than dialogs. Doesn't see it as partnership.	Sees parents as potential partners to help student. Has regular communication with parents. Adjusts without judgment for limitations of some parents.	Highly regarded by parents in community. Often requested as teacher. Works to create partnership with parents. Communicates regularly and appropriately.

Source: *Developing Expertise and Rigor* by R. K. Payne, 2013.

Collegial relationships

For under-resourced students to succeed academically, collegial relationships are essential among teachers, administrators, and staff members. Everyone needs to be on the same page about how the school will address the issues faced by these students at risk.

Many schools use PLCs (professional learning communities), and that's a wonderful tool to encourage collegiality. But if those meetings aren't carefully structured with an accountability piece, they often are mostly a waste of time. One of the questions I asked myself when I was a principal was: "How much are we complaining or pooling ignorance versus talking about and analyzing student work?"

PLC's can identify under-resourced adolescents, keeping each other in the loop on those students' status, and collaboratively develop strategies for coaching those students as well as providing support.

Training that builds the capacity of the parent as an individual

Under-resourced students can be successful academically if there is district level support for parent training that builds the capacity of the parent as an individual. Currently, most of the parent training that is done in schools with under-resourced parents is ineffective because parents who are most in need of it usually don't show up at school. Also, parent training almost always focuses on the child rather than the adult, but parents must first learn about themselves—knowledge almost always begins with oneself. My research and experience has resulted in a co-investigation training approach in which we give parents information and they discuss its application to their lives. This information they discuss includes: predators, resources, future stories, an analysis of community resources, rules about money, the use of language, hidden rules at work and school, causes of poverty and what can be done individually to shift their own situations. In other words, it is information about themselves. It is virtually impossible to support their children's development of a future story if parents themselves don't have one.

In the last 12 years, my company, aha! Process, has trained more than 15,000 adults in poverty with a 15-lesson series called *Getting Ahead in a Just-Gettin'-By World* (DeVol, 2012). Typically the school district pays for the training out of Title One funds, and individual businesses, utility companies, grants, etc. pay the parents for participating (a $25 gift card per training). After going through this experience, the difference for almost all of them in their attitude toward education and schooling—and the way they support their children—is phenomenal. They become much more supportive of school. As a grandmother in Memphis told me, "I raised two boys. Now I am raising my grandsons. I did not know you should talk about going to college with your kids. I did not know that they need a future story. I did not know how to help them build their own resources. I did not know why grades were so important. I did not do it for my sons, but I do it for my grandsons and I tell them why they need it."

Community involvement

To get bond levies passed, support staff development, and fund extra-curricular activities and advisory classes, the school district must engage and *educate* the larger community. Consider these facts: in 1960, nearly half (49%) of U.S. households had school-age children. In 2012, only 29% had school-age children—a lot fewer voters had a "direct line" to the school. Yet the need for support is great: In 2010, about 22% of children lived in households that were food insecure at times (Federal Interagency Forum on Child and Family Statistics, 2012, p. 7). The school district must communicate the needs of the under-resourced and lead in inspiring the community to step up and share and develop resources so that all their children succeed, thus enriching the community.

Many schools in other communities shut the door on visitors for safety reasons and fear that visitors will see something that gets reported to the community in a negative way. But isolation breeds mistrust and misinformation. You must find a safe way to bring the community into the school and the school into the community. The reason that community involvement and engagement are so necessary is that the people who have the political clout and who actually vote have very little knowledge and involvement about schools—unless there is a concerted effort to welcome them and inform them.

The reality, in short, is clear: Communities cannot be sustainable in the long term without involvement from a broad spectrum of community people.

CONCLUSION

The message of the research is unmistakable. Success in life is inextricably linked to success at the middle level. Because these years are so incredibly formative—in all stages of development discussed in this book—it's essential for adolescents to have a foundation of individuation, identification of self, and how they are alike and different from their parents and friends. The adults to whom they have access, along with the understandings, knowledge, and interests that they acquire, set the stage for the rest of their life—and the adults they are becoming.

When I have an individual who tells me it isn't important to fund or particularly pay attention to students at the middle level, and I realize that person isn't motivated by altruism, I ask these questions (appealing instead to pragmatism):

Do you want to keep the funding going to your school because your ADA (average daily attendance) is high? Do you want to bring jobs into your community so that you can keep your real estate values high? Do you want to keep your grandchildren close to you? Then, invest in students at the middle level. A healthy adolescence is the cornerstone of a lifetime of success.

And so, when you as an educator are discouraged, please remember that the gift you bring to students is not only about today, it's about the future. And it's the future not only of the student but of our well-being and viability as a nation. Teaching is a multi-generational activity. Our students teach their children, and so it continues. It's the Johnny Appleseed story: planting the seeds now for future growth and development.

When that teaching is done from a stance of safety, belonging, understanding, and expertise, there is no greater gift.

BIBLIOGRAPHY

Ablow, K. (2007). *Living the truth.* New York, NY: Little, Brown.

Ainsworth, M. D. S., & Bowlby, J. (1991). An ethological approach to personality development. *American Psychologist, 46,* 331–341.

Arrien, A. (1993). *The four-fold way: Walking the paths of warrior, teacher, healer and visionary.* New York, NY: HarperCollins.

Balfanz, R. (2009). *Putting middle grades students on the graduation path: A policy and practice brief.* Westerville, OH: National Middle School Association.

Bates, T. (2012, April 19). Speech given in Dublin, Ireland. *Sustaining the person of the leader.* Presentation at Leading in a Time of Challenge: Sustaining the Leader to Sustain the Child. Dublin, Ireland.

Berger, K. S. (2011). *The developing person through the life span* (8th ed.). New York, NY: Worth.

Berliner, D. C. (2009). Poverty and potential: Out-of-school factors and school success. National Education Policy Center. Retrieved from http://nepc.colorado.edu/publication/poverty-and-potential

Bowlby, J. (1969). *Attachment: Attachment and loss* (Vol. 1). New York, NY: Basic Books.

Bowlby, J. (1973). *Separation, anxiety, and anger: Attachment and loss* (Vol. 2). New York, NY: Basic Books.

Bowlby, J. (1980). *Loss: Sadness and depression.* New York, NY: Basic Books.

Brown, K. (August, 2011). Shocking need: American kids go hungry. Retrieved from http://abcnews.go.com/US/hunger_at_home/hunger-home-american-children-malnourished/story?id=14367230

Brown, P. M. (2013). Advocacy through advisory. In P. G. Andrews (Ed.), *Research to guide practice in middle grades education* (pp. 571-590). Westerville, OH: Association for Middle Level Education.

Byron, K., & Mitchell, S. (2002). *Loving what is: Four questions that can change your life.* New York, NY: Three Rivers Press.

Carnes, P. J. (1997). *The betrayal bond: Breaking free of exploitive relationships.* Deerfield Beach, FL: Health Communications.

Centers for Disease Control and Prevention (CDC). (2007). Adolescent health in the United States, 2007. Retrieved from http://www.cdc.gov/nchs/data/misc/adolescent2007.pdf

Clark, R. C. (2008). *Building expertise: Cognitive methods for training and performance improvement* (3rd ed.). San Francisco, CA: Pfeiffer.

Comer, J. (1995). Lecture given at Education Service Center, Region IV, Houston, TX.

Colby, A., Kohlberg, L., Gibbs, J., & Lieberman, M. (1983). A longitudinal study of moral judgment. *Monographs of the Society for Research in Child Development, 48*(1–2, Serial No. 200), 1–96.

Coleman-Jensen, A., Nord, M., Andrews, M., & Carlson, S. (2011, September). Household food security in the United States in 2010 [summary]. Retrieved from http://www.ers.usda.gov/media/121066/err125_reportsummary.pdf

Crosnoe, R., & Johnson, M. K. (2011). Research on adolescence in the 21st century. *Annual Review of Sociology, 37*, 439–460. doi:10.1146/annurev-soc-081309-150008

Dahl, R. E., & Speak, L. P. (2004). *Adolescent brain development: Vulnerabilities and opportunities.* New York, NY: The New York Academy of Sciences.

DeVol, P. E. (2012). *Getting ahead in a just-gettin'-by world: Building your resources for a better life* (revised ed.). Highlands, TX: aha! Process.

Dickey, D. D. (2013). *Graphic organizers and instructional snapshots for Common Core Standards.* Baltimore, MD: Educational Epiphany.

Dooley, B., & Fitzgerald, A. (2012). My world survey: National study of youth mental health in Ireland. Headstrong—The National Centre for Youth Mental Health and UCD School of Psychology. Retrieved from http://www.headstrong.ie/sites/default/files/My%20World%20Survey%202012%20Online.pdf

Dunphy, D. (1963). The social structure of urban adolescent peer groups. *Sociometry, 26*, 230–246.

Dweck, C. (2006). *Mindset: The new psychology of success.* New York, NY: Random House.

Eisenberg, N. (1986). *Altruistic emotion, cognition, and behavior.* Hillsdale, NJ: Erlbaum.

Elkind, D. (1967). Egocentrism in adolescence. *Child Development, 38,* 1025–1034.

Elkind, D. (2007). *The power of play: How spontaneous, imaginative activities lead to happier, healthier children.* Cambridge, MA: Da Capo Press.

Erikson, E. H. (1950). *Childhood and society.* New York, NY: Norton.

Erikson, E. H. (1968). *Identity, youth, and crisis.* New York, NY: Norton.

Etcoff, N., Orbach, S., Scott, J., & D'Agostino, H. (2004). The real truth about beauty: A global report. Retrieved from http://www.clubofamsterdam.com/contentarticles/52%20Beauty/dove_white_paper_final.pdf

Fassler, D. G., & Dumas, L. S. (1997). *Help me, I'm sad: Recognizing, treating, and preventing childhood and adolescent depression.* New York, NY: Penguin Books.

Federal Interagency Forum on Child and Family Statistics. (2012). America's children in brief: Key national indicators of well-being, 2012. Retrieved from http://www.childstats.gov/pdf/ac2012/ac_12.pdf

Feuerstein, R., Rand, Y., Hoffman, M. B., & Miller, R. (1980). *Instrumental enrichment: An intervention program for cognitive modifiability.* Glenview, IL: Scott, Foresman.

Friedman, E. H. (2007). *A failure of nerve: Leadership in the age of the quick fix.* New York, NY: Seabury Books.

Galambos, N. L., Barker, E. V., & Tilton-Weaver, L. C. (2003). Canadian adolescents' implicit theories of immaturity: What does 'childish' mean? *New Directions for Child and Adolescent Development, 100,* 77–90.

Giedd, J. N. (2009, February 26). The teen brain: Primed to learn, primed to take risks. *Cerebrum.* Retrieved from https://www.dana.org/news/cerebrum/detail.aspx?id=19620

Greenspan, S. I., & Benderly, B. L. (1997). *The growth of the mind: And the endangered origins of intelligence.* Cambridge, MA: Da Capo Press.

Hart, B., & Risley, T. R. (1995). *Meaningful differences in the everyday experience of young American children.* Baltimore, MD: Paul H. Brookes.

Hopson, L. M., & Lee, E. (2011). Mitigating the effect of family poverty on academic and behavioral outcomes: The role of school climate in middle and high school. *Children and Youth Services Review, 33*(11), 2221–2229.

Karpman, S. (1968). Fairy tales and script drama analysis. *Transactional Analysis Bulletin, 7*(26), 39–43.

Karpman, S. (1974). Overlapping egograms. *Transactional Analysis Journal, 4*(4), 16–19.

Kennedy, R. (n.d.). Karpman's drama triangle. Noeticus Counseling Center and Training Institute. Retrieved from http://www.noeticus.org/uploads/Handout-Karpman_s_ Drama_Triangle-Color.pdf

Kishiyama, M. M., Boyce, W. T., Jimenez, A. M., Perry, L. M., & Knight, R. T. (2009). Socioeconomic disparities affect prefrontal function in children. *Journal of Cognitive Neuroscience, 21*(6), 1106–1115. Doi:10.1162/jocn.2009.21101

Kohlberg, L. (1981). *The philosophy of moral development: Moral stages and the idea of justice.* San Francisco, CA: Harper and Row.

Kohlberg, L. (1984). *Essays on moral development, Volume II: The psychology of moral development.* San Francisco, CA: Harper and Row.

Lareau, A. (2003). *Unequal childhoods: Class, race, and family life.* Berkeley, CA: University of California Press.

Levine, A., & Heller, R. S. F. (2011, January/February). Get attached: The surprising secrets to finding the right partner for a healthy relationship. *Scientific American Mind,* 22–29.

Lounsbury, J. H.., Carson, S. T., & Andrews, P. G. (2013). Looping and multiage grouping: Providing long-term student-teacher relationships—and time. In P. G. Andrews (Ed.), *Research to guide practice in middle grades education* (pp. 633–675). Westerville, OH: Association for Middle Level Education.

Love, P., & Stosny, S. (2007). *How to improve your marriage without talking about it: Finding love beyond words.* New York, NY: Broadway.

Main, M., & Solomon, J. (1986). Discovery of an insecure-disorganized/disoriented attachment pattern. In T. B. Brazelton and M. W. Yogman, *Affective development in infancy* (pp. 95–124). Norwood, NJ: Ablex.

Maslow, A. H. (1943). A theory of human motivation. *Psychological Review, 50,* 370–396.

McEwin, C. K., & Smith, T. W. (2013). The professional preparation of middle grades teachers. In P. G. Andrews (Ed.), R*esearch to guide practice in middle grades education* (pp. 679–695). Westerville, OH: Association for Middle Level Education.

McLeod, S. A. (2007). Maslow's hierarchy of needs. *Simply Psychology.* Retrieved from http://www.simplypsychology.org/maslow.html

Monastersky, R. (2007). Who's minding the teenage brain? *Chronicle of higher education, 53*(19), A14–A18.

National Middle School Association. (2010). *This we believe: Keys to educating young adolescents.* Westerville, OH: Author.

Oberle, E., & Schonert-Reichl, K. A. (2013). Relations among peer acceptance, inhibitory control, and math achievement in early adolescence. *Journal of Applied Developmental Psychology, 34*(1), 45–51.

Olweus, D., Limber, S. P., & Mihalic, S. (1999). *The bullying prevention program: Blueprints for violence prevention, Volume 10.* Boulder, CO: Center for the Study and Prevention of Violence.

Palincsar, A. S., & Brown, A. L. (1984). The reciprocal teaching of comprehension-fostering and comprehension-monitoring activities. *Cognition and Instruction, 1*(2), 117–175.

Parker, J., & Benson, M. (2004). Parent-adolescent relations and adolescent functioning: Self-esteem, substance abuse, and delinquency. Europe PubMed Central. http://europepmc.org/abstract/MED/15673227/reload=0;jsessionid=k9iJOp5t5UU3 aq8Ce5mo.6

Payne, R. K. (2008). *Under-resourced learners: 8 strategies to boost student achievement.* Highlands, TX: aha! Process.

Payne, R. K. (2009). *Research-based strategies: Narrowing the achievement gap for under-resourced students.* Highlands, TX: aha! Process.

Payne, R. K. (2013). *A framework for understanding poverty: A cognitive approach.* Highlands, TX: aha! Process.

Payne, R. K. (2013). *Developing expertise and rigor* [report prepared for Texas Association of School Administrators]. Highlands, TX: aha! Process.

Payne, R. K. (in press). *How much of yourself do you own? A handbook for developing emotional resources.* Highlands, TX: aha! Process.

Payne, R. K. (in process). *Building student expertise and rubrics.* Highlands, TX: aha! Process.

Piaget, J. (2009). La causalité chez l'enfant (Children's understanding of causality). *British Journal of Psychology, 100*(S1), 207–224. doi:10.1348/000712608X336059

Ratey, J. J. (2008). S*park: The Revolutionary New Science of Exercise and the Brain.* New York, NY: Little, Brown.

Revoy, M. (2011, February 9). Teenagers shot for developing their thinking. *Now I get it! Understanding the adolescent brain* [blog]. Retrieved from http://understandingtheadolescentbrain.blogspot.com/search/label/Cognitive%20Development%3B

Richo, D. (2002). *How to be an adult in relationships: The five keys to mindful loving.* London, England: Shambala.

Satir, V. (1972). *Peoplemaking.* Palo Alto, CA: Science and Behavior Books.

Schurr, S. (2012). *Authentic assessment: Active, engaging, product and performance measures.* Westerville, OH: Association for Middle Level Education.

Shanahan, L., McHale, S. M., Osgood, D. W., & Crouter, A. C. (2007). Conflict frequency with mothers and fathers from middle childhood to late adolescence: Within- and between-families comparisons. *Developmental Psychology, 43,* 539–550.

Sharron, H., & Coulter, M. (2004). *Changing children's minds: Feuerstein's revolution in the teaching of intelligence* (4th ed.). Highlands, TX: aha! Process.

Silver, Debbie. (2012). *Fall down 7 times get up 8.* Thousand Oaks, CA; Westerville, OH: Corwin; Association for Middle Level Education.

Smetana, J. G. (2010). *Adolescents, families, and social development: How teens construct their worlds.* Hoboken, NJ: Wiley-Blackwell.

Smith, C., & Denton, M. L. (2005). *Soul searching: The religious and spiritual lives of American teenagers.* Oxford, United Kingdom: Oxford University Press.

Spencer, J. (2008). *Everyone's invited: Interactive strategies that engage young adolescents.* Westerville, OH: National Middle School Association.

Spencer, J. (2012). *Ten differentiation strategies for building prior knowledge.* Westerville, OH: Association for Middle Level Education.

Spencer, J. (2013). *Ten differentiation strategies for building Common Core literacy.* Westerville, OH: Association for Middle Level Education.

Thompson, K. F. (2013). Service-Learning: Connecting curriculum to community. In P. G. Andrews (Ed.), *Research to guide practice in middle grades education* (pp. 247–265). Westerville, OH: Association for Middle Level Education.

Thorsborne, M., & Vinegrad, D. (2009). *Restorative justice pocketbook.* Alresford, United Kingdom: Teachers' Pocketbooks.

Tough, P. (2012). *How children succeed: Grit, curiosity, and the hidden power of character.* Boston, MA: Houghton Mifflin Harcourt.

Trotter, K. S. (n.d.). *Task of childhood.* Retrieved from http://www.kaytrotter.com/Forms/ Task_of_Childhood.pdf

Williams, K. D. (2011). The pain of exclusion. *Scientific American Mind, 21,* 30–37. doi:10.1038/scientificamericanmind0111-30

Woititz, J. G. (1990). *Adult children of alcoholics.* Deerfield Beach, FL: HCI Books.

Young, K. (2013, April 22). Dove's new beauty campaign confirms that we are more beautiful than we think. Retrieved from http://fashion.telegraph.co.uk/beauty/ news-features/TMG10009657/Doves-new-beauty-campaign-confirms-that-we- are-more-beautiful-than-we-think.html

Zimbardo, P. G., & Duncan, N. (2012, May 24). " 'The Demise of Guys': How video games and porn are ruining a generation." Retrieved from http://www.cnn.com/2012/05/23/health/living-well/demise-of-guys